COURTROOM
CRACK

COURTROOM CRACK

Compiled by Scott Learmonth
Foreword by Joe Beltrami S.S.C.
and Donald R Findlay Q.C.

Neil Wilson Publishing ● Glasgow

Published by Neil Wilson Publishing Ltd
309 The Pentagon Centre
36 Washington Street
GLASGOW G3 8AZ
Tel: 041-221-1117
Fax: 041-221-5363

A catalogue record for this book is available from the British Library.
ISBN 1-897784-24-4

Typeset in 12/14pt Palatino by Face to Face Design Services, Glasgow

Printed in Musselburgh by Scotprint Ltd

Contents

Foreword

The criminal courts are not normally places which are associated with humour. People go there to be punished or hopefully acquitted; they are summoned as witnesses and asked questions by lawyers who treat them as if they are either liars or just downright stupid; or they are required to sit as jurors and pronounce upon the guilt or innocence of their fellow men and women. The proceedings are presided over by an ancient looking judge sporting a horsehair wig. Man's inhumanity to man provides the daily bread for the criminal lawyer.

Yet it is against this background that humour can and does flourish. People who are forced into an alien environment and questioned in public, often find that the mouth and brain become disengaged.

An accused who had survived cross-examination for over an hour, fell at the last hurdle. The prosecutor's last question ran thus: 'To claim that you were at home with your dog when ten people identify you as robbing the bank is not a very good story is it?' He answered, with engaging honesty, 'Right enough, my lawyer said it was a load of rubbish'.

Lawyers are not immune from the verbal foot in the mouth. An eminent prosecuting counsel once asked a witness: 'Are you Mohammed Abdullah Frib?'

He received the answer: 'Yes, I am Mohammed Abdullah. Yes, I am a Fellow of the Royal Institute of Biologists'.

Representing a client involves a heavy responsibility and is necessarily a serious business. However, moments of humour provide invaluable relief from the strains of the job.

An accused who had pled guilty to the charge against him was asked by the judge if he had a lawyer. He replied, 'I don't want a lawyer. I want to tell the truth'.

A counsel listened to his client's story and explained, 'I think it would be proper to plead alibi in this case'. His client responded irately, 'Ah'm no pleading alibi. Ah'm innocent!'.

However strong the Crown case may be, there are always clients who seem determined to make it stronger. An Irishman accused of rape was required to stand on an identification parade. When the bruised and battered victim entered the room the accused leaped forward and pronounced, 'To be sure, that's the very wumman — yes that's her, I swear it!'

Courtroom crack has always interested the public at large and a compendium such as this should be food and drink to its aficionados. These court stories go back more than 150 years to an era when Bridewell and not Bar-L was the principal guest house of Her Majesty.

Herald diarist Tom Shields move over — here we have a litany of courtroom stories, from the mildly amusing to the very funny, but all vouched as authentic. A great deal of research has gone into Scott Learmonth's compilation of this unique book. We thoroughly enjoyed it and are confident that the reader will find it a source of entertainment and delight. This opinion we give freely — a rarity for lawyers!

Joseph Beltrami S.S.C.
Donald R. Findlay Q.C.

The Unusual

GLASGOW ARGUS   25TH APRIL 1833

William Telfer, pleaded guilty to a charge of bigamy having first married a female in the parish of Preston, England, some years ago, and, while she was in life, betaken to himself a second spouse somewhere about Blantyre. Panel instructed his Counsel to say that he was exceedingly sorry for what he had done, — and that one of the marriages had been contracted while he was in a state of intoxication. Neither in England nor Scotland would a marriage be solemnized unless the banns had been previously proclaimed — so that the prisoner must have indulged in a state of intoxication for a length of time. However his Lordship felt inclined to limit his punishment to nine months confinement in the County Bridewell at hard labour.

GLASGOW ARGUS   1ST JANUARY 1835

A young lad, a baker, was on Monday forenoon charged in the Police Court with behaving in an indecorous manner in a place of worship occupied by the Primitive Methodists or Ranters. It was proved in evidence, and indeed admitted by the defender, that he had laughed outright during the progress of the service, and by so doing tickled various others, who unable to resist the infection joined in the laugh. The defender was, after an admonition from Bailie Craig, fined 10s 6d.

GLASGOW ARGUS   *7TH AUGUST 1837*

A boy was sentenced to Bridewell recently by the Justices of the Peace for stealing a pair of breeches belonging to a soldier, which breeches were declared in the Commitment to be the property of Her Majesty Queen Victoria the First.

GLASGOW SATURDAY POST   *27TH JANUARY 1844*

Miss Roalfe was yesterday placed at the bar of the Sheriff Court, charged with vending profane and blasphemous works at her shop, 103 Nicolson Street. She pled not guilty. Miss Roalfe, who conducted her own defence, made a long statement to the Court in which she admitted the sale of the works, libelled, knowing perfectly that they contained a denial of the truth of the Christian religion, and were calculated to bring it into contempt, but denied that she considered her conduct criminal, that so soon as she should be a liberty she intended to resume the same practice. Mr Tait, the presiding Sheriff having found the charge proven, sentenced her to 60 days imprisonment.

GLASGOW SATURDAY POST   *27TH APRIL 1844*

A respectable member of the Baptist Church in Dunfermline, being last week a witness in a case before the Sheriff, refused to take the oath, from conscientious scruples, regarding Christ's command 'swear not at all'. He was sentenced to two days imprisonment in jail for contempt of court — a sentence which was fully carried into execution.

GLASGOW SATURDAY POST   *24TH MAY 1845*

In the Police Court on Wednesday, No.121 city porter, was fined 5s for refusing to act in that capacity to Messrs McTear and Kempt, auctioneers, he being at the time unengaged.

GLASGOW SATURDAY POST   *22ND NOVEMBER 1845*

Four men and three women were on Monday charged at the Police Court with desecrating the Sabbath, by dancing, whistling and playing upon a trumpet in a house in Back Wynd betwixt the hours of two and three o'clock on the morning of Sabbath last. The tenant of the house was fined in one guinea; and the other parties dismissed.

GLASGOW SATURDAY POST   *2ND OCTOBER 1847*

James Blair, John Porter and John McGregor, Perth, were on Monday last brought before Mr Barclay and Bailie Greig, as Justices of the Peace, charged, at the instance of the Fiscal, with profaning the Sabbath, in contravention of the Scots Act 1661, chap 18, by fishing with nets and cables in the River Tay at an early hour of Sabbath the 22nd day of August last. The

Justices found the parties liable in the penalty of ten pounds Scotch each, according to the Act.

GLASGOW SATURDAY POST   14TH JULY 1849

A chimney-sweeper named Macpherson and a respectable looking female, named Dick, residing in Castle Street, were charged with having, on the 30th of June last, permitted a young boy, about nine years of age, to go up a chimney in the house of the latter, in contravention of the Act, specially referring to the offence. The boy, it appears, is in the employment of Macpherson, and had been hired, along with another lad, to sweep a vent in Mrs Dick's house. The fact, of the boy having been in the chimney being clearly established, the Bailie imposed a fine of two guineas on Macpherson and half a guinea on Mrs Dick.

GLASGOW EXAMINER   19TH MARCH 1859

On Monday, before James Craig, Esq and James King, Esq, Justices, Michael O'Houn, jun, and Daniel Bradly, apprentices with Messrs Wm. Murray and Co. Caledonian Bottle Works, pleaded guilty to having deserted their employment and were each sent to prison for three months.

GLASGOW EXAMINER   21ST JULY 1860

Hugh Matheson, was charged with causing an obstruction at the junction of St Vincent Place and Buchanan Street, by exhibiting a live rat.

The Bailie dismissed the accused, remarking on the novelty of the case, and advising Matheson to find a more proper place than the public street for his rat exhibition.

GLASGOW EXAMINER   *21ST JULY 1860*

Barney McManus was charged with slaughtering a goat in a close in Saltmarket. The wife of McManus who appeared to answer the charge admitted the offence, but with real Irish sincerity, assured his Honour that the goat had been in the way of dying for the last six weeks and was just killed to see what was the matter with it. The woman was dismissed with the admonition that next when she had a goat to slaughter to convey it to the proper place.

GLASGOW EXAMINER   *28TH JANUARY 1866*

At the Central Police Court on Tuesday a man named John Watson, Saltmarket, was fined a guinea, with the alternative of 15 days imprisonment, for throwing an orange skin on the pavement in the Trongate on the 23rd instant. As he could not pay the fine he was sent to prison.

RUTHERGLEN REFORMER   *9TH JUNE 1877*

For allowing or causing to be laid, manure on the street after regulation hours, Peter Harvies, North Bridge Street, was fined 2s 6d.

A woman named Mrs Butler residing at 86 King Street, was charged with a contravention of the Public Health Act, in so far as she had been keeping lodgers in her house without a certificate. It came out in evidence that when the inspector had paid a visit to the house he found no fewer than 15 persons all lodged in a small room and kitchen.

She was fined 10s or 5 days in prison, and warned that if she was again charged with a similar offence the penalty would be much more serious.

At the fortnightly Burgh Court, held on Monday last, Bailie Sutherland presiding, John Thom, police constable, residing at the Police Station, Bathgate, pled guilty to a charge (given in by himself) of causing the chimney of the Police Office to catch or be on fire, and was fined in the statutory penalty of 2s 6d.

A woman named Marjory Docherty or Kerr, Walker Street, was fined £15 with £1 13s 6d of expenses — the alternative being three months imprisonment — for selling whisky without a licence in her house, on the morning of Sunday last. The charge was aggravated by it being her second offence. Sergeant McPherson had been passing the house at an early hour on Sunday morning and heard a dispute about the payment of a round, and on going into the place he apprehended three women, who had begun to fight among themselves.

GOVAN CHRONICLE & PARTICK OBSERVER   21ST JUNE 1878

Peter Flannigan, a labourer, residing in Logie Street, and Bernard McLuskey, another labourer, were placed at the bar on a charge of contravening the Act for the Prevention of Cruelty to Animals, by having on Saturday, on a piece of ground between Broomloan Road and Queen Street, encouraged or aided at the fighting of two cocks belonging to them. The Magistrate, in passing sentence, said it was clearly proven that they were both what they called in Scotland 'egging' them on to fight each other and imposed a fine of l0s 6d or ten days.

GLASGOW WEEKLY HERALD   *18TH OCTOBER 1879*

At the Central Police Court on Thursday before Stipendiary Gemmel — a hackney carriage driver named Thomas Miller was charged with contravening by-law 26 of the Glasgow Police Act, he having on the cab stand at George Square fed his horse 'with hay otherwise than from his hand'. Miller pleaded guilty. The Magistrate said this was the first case of the kind that had came before him, and he would not therefore impose any penalty. Cab drivers, however, had better take a warning, because he would certainly deal differently with the next case.

AIRDRIE ADVERTISER   *27TH MARCH 1880*

On Thursday at the Airdrie J.P. Court, before, Mr A Aitken and Dr Wilson, David Clark and John Goudie, miners, Bellshill, were found guilty of falsely representing that they were bona fide travellers on Sunday the 14 inst, to the landlord of the Railway Hotel at Bellshill, and so got supplied with a gill of whisky and a pint of ale. They were fined 40s, with the alternative of 15 days imprisonment.

GLASGOW WEEKLY NEWS   *25TH FEBRUARY 1882*

KILMARNOCK — On Monday the presiding Magistrates, Bailies Wilson and McLelland, were presented with a pair of white gloves each on the occasion of their being not a single prisoner to try. It is nearly twenty years since a similar event occurred.

Thomas Ballantyne, miner, Marshall Street was next called. Mrs Ballantyne appeared, and in extenuation pled that her boy Samuel complained of bad ears. He was a 'guid skolar' and it was the first complaint against him. On being reminded that she had been frequently before the board for irregular attendance of her children, she retorted 'Oh aye, but no for that one, I cannae help it.'

The Chairman: 'The boy is nine and a-half years of age, and is only in the second standard and has just made fifteen out of forty attendances at school.'

Mrs Ballantyne: 'I didna ken he had dune so bad; but I hae gien him a guid fright.'

Major Williams: 'Do you give him a good wigging?'

Mrs Ballantyne: 'I didna ken what ye say, sir.'

The Major: 'Do you give him a good thrashing?'

Mrs Ballantyne replied in the affirmative. Mr Frew advised her to try something else.

Mrs Ballantyne: 'There's many a time he keeps greetin' a' nicht wi' his sair ears, an' is no able to gang to skule.'

On being further admonished Mrs Ballantyne left muttering that her next door neighbours had weans that were nae scholars and the skule board said nothing to them.

School Board Officer: 'The next door neighbour appears next Mr Chairman.'

GLASGOW WEEKLY HERALD   *9TH SEPTEMBER 1882*

On Wednesday, 16 members of the Salvation Army in Forfar, including the 'Captain' and 'Lieutenant' were apprehended and taken to the Police Office on a charge of breaking the public peace and singing and shouting on the public thoroughfares and with collecting a very large crowd of people. The names and addresses of the whole sixteen were taken down, and Mr Stirling liberated them on a promise that until the charge had been disposed of they will not repeat the offence.

RUTHERGLEN REFORMER &
CAMBUSLANG JOURNAL   *8TH MAY 1885*

James Dailly, residing at 100 Main Street was charged with the crime of assault committed on Saturday night. In evidence it was stated that the accused had assaulted one of the Constables while in the discharge of his public duty, and that an exceedingly large crowd of people had been collected on the street in consequence of the conduct of Dailly and a number of his companions.

A considerable quantity of stones had been thrown at the police, and finding a scarcity of these missiles one of the crowd picked up a dog who happened to be in the way and violently threw it at the heads of the constables.

After commenting upon the seriousness of the charge, the presiding Magistrate inflicted a fine of 21s, or 10 days imprisonment.

SOUTH SUBURBAN PRESS   *26TH MARCH 1887*

At the Govanhill Police Court, last Monday morning — Bailie Copestake on the bench — Alexander Eadie, builder, residing at Inglefield, Pollockshields, was fined 20s or fourteen days imprisonment for allowing a ferocious dog to be at large. From the evidence it appeared that the dog, a black and tan collie, had entered the yard of Mr McTurk, cabinet maker, Allison Street, on Saturday 12 inst., and while there, bit one of the apprentices on the arm, taking the piece out. It had also knocked down a little boy earlier in the day and bit him on the head and hand. About a month previous it had bitten a young lady on the arm in Pollockshields. A number of witnesses were examined, and one for the defence, stated that he considered that playfulness on the part of the dog was all that was the matter.

GOVAN PRESS   *21ST MAY 1887*

On Thursday, 12th inst., Thomas Jackson, engineer, Muirkirk, Ayrshire, attempted to commit suicide by drinking a quantity of laudanum in Fairfield Street. He was brought before Bailie Marr and the day following fined 10s 6d, with the alternative of seven days imprisonment as a lesson that life is still worth living.

GOVAN PRESS   *16TH JULY 1887*

William Neeson, labourer, 158 Main Street, Maryhill, pleaded guilty to having had a flower pot on the outside sill of his window and not properly fastened. It appears the pot had been blown off by the wind and fell on a woman's head. He was fined in 2s 6d or three days inprisonment.

SOUTH SUBURBAN PRESS   *12TH MAY 1888*

Mary McMillan, a charwoman, Annie Laurie, domestic servant, Leven Street, Pollokshields and Margaret Park, charwoman, were charged with beating carpets in Melville Street. They pled guilty and after being reprimanded were dismissed. They were told to go in future to the vacant ground in the vicinity as beating carpets on the street was a violation of the Police Act.

Govan Press   *9th June 1888*

Matthew Smith, hammerman, Douglas Street and Wm Fisher, engineer, 2 Merryland Street, Govan, each forfeited a pledge of 15s by failing to answer a charge of assaulting Helen Donnelly or McCall, 30 Anderson Street, in Anderson Street, by kissing her late on Saturday night or early on Sunday morning.

South Suburban Press   *8th September 1888*

When the new toy gun, known as the potato gun, was introduced fear was expressed by several who knew something of what boys will do, that to keep the youngsters in amusement, grocers' potato barrels would suffer. This has unfortunately been verified in our midst. Three boys of tender years were on Monday last brought forward at Govanhill Police Court on a charge of stealing potatoes from the door of a shop in the neighbourhood, and their parents in answer said it was not the boys that were to blame but those who sold the guns as the temptation to steal was greatly increased by the introduction of such a toy. The boys were dismissed with an admonition.

Wishaw Press   *16th February 1889*

Peter McCormick, miner, Logans Row, was charged with staggering in an intoxicated state, in Main Street, on Sunday afternoon. He vigorously denied the accusation. Constables Smith and Taylor gave evidence to the effect that they had seen him coming down the footpath in a very erratic manner and holding on by the wall occasionally. Bailie Russell remarked that in circumstances such as these some test might be applied to ascertain whether a man was drunk or not and suggested the expendient of making a prisoner walk a 9 inch plank on being taken to the office. The charge against McCormick he found not proven.

POLLOCKSHAWS NEWS   *12TH APRIL 1889*

Samuel Abraham, residing in Coustonhill Street, was charged with failing to provide education for his son, Samuel. Samuel had been very troublesome for the past 4 years. Out of a possible attendance of 208 since last October, his total reached 9. Mr Abraham said he had done his best with the boy. He was not a bad boy, but he could not be made to stay at school. He had taken him there himself often, but immediately on being released at 'piece' time he 'skedaddled' again. The Court continued the case till 2nd June warning Samuel that if he did not begin at once to go to school and to stay there he would probably be sent to an Industrial School for 3 years. Samuel promised he would.

RUTHERGLEN REFORMER   *28TH JUNE 1889*

Two boys, Henry Hill and Bernard Lafferty, residing in Low Coats, were accused of stealing a joiner's and plasterer's hammer from a house in the course of erection in Low Coats. Hill pleaded guilty of taking one hammer, and Lafferty pleaded that he was in the company but did not take any hammer. The first plea was accepted, and the charge in Lafferty's case was found not proven. Hill was fined half a crown or 24 hours, and his mother ordered to give him a good whipping.

GLASGOW WEEKLY MAIL   *30TH AUGUST 1890*

LINLITHGOW — At the Sheriff Court on Wednesday, Elizabeth McGarrol, an old woman, was sentenced to ten days imprisonment for throwing herself into the Firth of Forth at Bo'ness on 10th August, with the intention of drowning herself. Accused explained that she 'was only washing her feet'.

GOVAN PRESS   *7TH FEBRUARY 1891*

James Campbell, labourer, Henderson Street, off New City Road, Glasgow, for disorderly conduct in Gairbraid Street, Eastpark on Tuesday night was fined 2s 6d. His wife Mary was fined in 2s 6d for being 'a wee bit the wau o' a dram' in the same street on the same night. Both got the alternative of 24 hours inprisonment. Campbell paid his fine and left to get cash to lift his wife, but not turning up in time Mrs Campbell was taken to prison. The guidman in the meantime seems to have got possession of some bawbees but appears to have forgotten all about his wife, as later on in the evening he was picked up in Wyndford Street, quite oblivious and again quartered in the police office.

GLASGOW HERALD   18TH DECEMBER 1891

James C Kinmead, tea planter, of Cardney in the parish of Caputh, was charged with having on 21st October last, employed seven male servants while he only had a licence for three. Mr Kinmead found it impossible through illness to attend the Court and proof was led in his absence. The charge was found proven and the respondent was fined in the modified penalty of £5. It was stated that Mrs Kinmead had taken out the licences.

POLLOCKSHAWS NEWS   11TH MARCH 1892

The redoubtable Thomas Robertson, chimney sweep, admitted being helplessly drunk on Saturday and was fined 5s or 24 hours imprisonment, the Fiscal remarking that he would be the better of a wash.

GLASGOW WEEKLY MAIL   12TH MARCH 1892

Warrant was granted by Bailies Nicol and McKenzie on Monday, for the destruction of a carcass of beef found in the premises of the Caledonian Railway Company, and belonging to James Johnstone, Hillhead Ironside, New Deer. Johnstone, the owner of the carcass, admitted in the witness box that the animal had been undergoing treatment, and that if it had not been killed it would have died.

The Procurator Fiscal (to the accused): 'You killed it to save its life?' *(laughter)*

Glasgow Weekly Herald   *11th June 1892*

At Pollockshaws Justice of Peace Court on Monday
— before Bailie Adam and Messrs Denholm and
Murdoch — five lads were charged with assaulting
a girl in Green Lane. The boys were playing at football, and, in the course of play, the ball struck the girl
on the head, fell among her feet and tripped her.
When she was down, the youths in their anxiety to
pursue the game, continued to kick, and the girl was
pretty severely abused. The Justices, after commenting strongly on the dangerous practice of playing
football on the streets, imposed fines on four of the
accused, and dismissed the other, the charge against
him not being proved.

Wishaw Press   *31st December 1892*

Felix Lyons, miner, Quarry Street, Hamilton, admitted having staggered under the influence of liquor

on Main Street on Sunday. He declared however, that he had only had twopence worth of beer and a glass of whisky, and he was not very drunk, for he could stand on one leg. The Fiscal asked if he had done that in the police office. Felix replied that he had, but could not say for how long. The Bailie remarked that the police might have tried his plan of making him walk the plank. The Fiscal in a bantering tone, told the accused it was very remarkable he could stand on one leg and could not walk on two, he should have remained standing on one leg in the street and not ventured to walk at all in any circumstances. The Assessor thought he would have been better at home eating his Christmas dinner. The prisoner was fined 10s or seven days imprisonment.

PARKHEAD, BRIDGETON, SHETTLESTON &
TOLLCROSS ADVERTISER   *APRIL 1893*

Mary McEwan, 639 Dalmarnock Road, was charged with having worked during the meal hour in the weaving factory of T.K.Kerr and Company, 9 Springfield Road, this being contrary to the Act. The rule alluded to was posted up in the works, and the employers exercised every reasonable care to have it respected. McEwan was fined 4s, with 1s of costs.

WISHAW PRESS   *5TH MAY 1894*

When Peter McVey, ironworker, Sunnyside Rows, was led forward to the bar, the Fiscal informed the Court that the man was deaf and dumb. The Inspector said he had not been able to find an interpreter. As it seemed impossible to make accused understand the nature of the charge preferred against him, the Fiscal handed his copy of the complaint to the Bench. After glancing over the document, the Assessor exclaimed: 'Are you sure this is the right complaint, Mr Burgess? I see this man is charged with cursing and swearing.' The Fiscal explained that McVey was accused of disorderly behaviour and without knowing that the man was deaf and dumb his clerk had evidently made out the complaint from the stereotyped copy. The charge was accordingly withdrawn and on the fact being communicated to the prisoner in writing he showed his appreciation of the kindness by appropriately saluting the Magistrate.

PARTICK & MARYHILL PRESS   *12TH MAY 1894*

Robert Dewart, a cordwainer, hailing from Glasgow, pled guilty of conducting himself in a disorderly manner on the north bank of the Clyde in the vicinity of Meadowside shipbuilding yard on Sunday last, and attempting to go into the river. The poor man was the worse of drink, and was inconsolable because all the pubs were closed, therefore he proposed to end his troubles with a big drink of Clyde water. He was fined 7s 6d or 5 days imprisonment.

AIRDRIE ADVERTISER   *30TH MAY 1893*

Before Bailie Knox — Thomas Spiers, labourer, 46 Shanks Street, was charged with overcrowding his house so as to be dangerous to the health of the inhabitants. He pleaded guilty. The Fiscal said the police found that the house consisted of a single apartment 10½ by 8 feet, in which 13 persons were found sleeping, including several who were not members of accused's family. He was fined 7s 6d or five days.

RUTHERGLEN REFORMER   *29TH JUNE 1894*

John Ferns, ironworker, Carrick Street, was charged with sitting on the sill of the public house window in Bank Street occupied by Mr John Benson, and stretching out his legs on the pavement, contrary to the Police Act, and after having been warned off by the police. The Bailie remarked that it was not a very well known offence, and he would let the man off this time, but cautioned him as to the future.

PARKHEAD, BRIDGETON, SHETTLESTON &
TOLLCROSS ADVERTISER   *JULY 1895*

Football on Sunday

Sir — I was pleased to see your correspondent drawing attention to the above disgraceful habit and it is certainly high time that our well paid guardians of the peace exerted themselves in endeavouring to root out the evil, for it shocks every right thinking man to know that it exists. I was an unfortunate witness to a game on the banks of Clyde last Sunday.

I am yours & C
CHURCHMAN

At the Northern Police Court on Tuesday a curious case was tried. A man named John Allison was charged with having worn the uniform of the 5th VBHLI in such a manner as to bring contempt upon such uniform, by riding on a donkey along Sauchiehall Street. The Judge said a more heinous violation of the Act had never come under his notice, and he fined Allison three guineas, with the alternative of 30 days imprisonment.

Five men and three women were remanded at the Glasgow Police Court on Monday, pending inquiry into a charge of having thrown James Buntine, a labourer from Duntocher, from the window of the house of James Houston, 29 Bridgegate, on Saturday afternoon. Having fallen from a height of two storeys, Buntine was very severely injured, and had to be taken to the Royal Infirmary for treatment. When he became conscious he stated that he was decoyed to this house by two women, but as he was the worse of drink he was unable to say what had been done to him.

Had his fall not been broken by his alighting on the top of an old woman who was passing at the time, it is very likely he would have been killed on the spot. The old woman received a wound on the head in addition to an injury to her neck.

RUTHERGLEN REFORMER   *10TH JULY 1896*

Joseph McGuiggan, Coatbank Street, was charged with malicious mischief, he having broken two panes of glass in the window of a house in 'Cat's Close'. A previous conviction for a similar offence was recorded against the accused.

The Bailie: 'How did you come to do this?'

Accused: 'A woman struck me on the head with a poker, and I was after her to let her have the same.' *(laughter)*

The Bailie: 'It's an awful Close that, surely it's high time some of our missionary folks were paying it a visit, it would be as good a field as many of them get abroad. *(laughter)* Fined 7s 6d or 5 days.'

RUTHERGLEN REFORMER   *14TH MAY 1897*

John Steadman, Crichton Street and James McCaull, Coat Street, were charged with quarrelling, and fighting in Main Street on Saturday night. Both accused had been previously convicted and had been fined 5s each.

The Bailie: 'It seems you want a little more this time, we'll pit a third on tae the last fine. 7s 6d or five days.'

GLASGOW EVENING NEWS   *22ND JUNE 1897*

At the Central Police Court there were 30 prisoners of whom 29 were liberated. There were 12 drunks, nine men and three women — and ex-Bailie Gray, who presided, asked all who would promise not to touch beer or whisky anymore to hold up their hands and he would let them go on account of this being the day of the Diamond Jubilee celebrations for the Queen. All the drunks held up their hands — except one, who was not yet capable — and only smiled — and they were liberated.

PARTICK STAR   *11TH DECEMBER 1897*

On Wednesday Bailie Porter fined four boys 2s 6d, or two days imprisonment each, for playing football on Sunday afternoon.

27TH MAY 1898

Edward Slavin, Coatbank Street and John Costelle, Iron Row, were charged with quarrelling and fighting in Coatbank Street on Saturday night. Both had previous convictions recorded against them. The Bailie, in view of the fact that he thought they were quiet looking fellows, restricted the penalty to one of 10s or seven days.

24TH FEBRUARY 1899

James Gourley, shingler, residing at 33 Russell Colt Street, was charged with a contravention of the Public House Prohibition Act, 1883, section 3, by paying Francis Croal, 23a Buchanan Street, his wages in Mclnlay's public house 132 Main Street on Saturday 4th February, about 3pm. The accused admitted the offence, but declared he was not aware of such an Act. Being the first case of the kind brought before the court, he was dismissed with admonition.

18TH MARCH 1899

Marion Simpson Strachan or Galbraith residing in Linthouse Buildings, was remitted to the Sheriff on a charge of having on 24th December 1890, in Fairfield U.P. Church, bigamously married Thomas Reid, shipplater, now deceased while her husband, William Galbraith, hammerman, also now deceased was alive.

17TH NOVEMBER 1899

At the Police Court on Monday — Bailie Logan on

the bench. Three lads named John Gray, John Graham and Hugh Fraser were charged with having loitered on the footway at Merkland Street, near Russell on the 5th inst. They pleaded not guilty and two Constables gave evidence in support of the charge. For the defence Mrs Graham said that she had seen the police taking her son 'for dain nothing'.

The charge was found proven — Bailie Logan said that this loitering was far too common. At the same time there were some other things which the police might look after. There was a 'darkey' in Dumbarton Road who nightly blocked up the thoroughfare at the head of Kelvin Street selling his quack medicines. Sentence of 5s or 3 days each was passed.

GLASGOW WEEKLY MAIL   20TH JANUARY 1900

At the Police Court on Monday — Provost Kirkwood on the bench — Mrs Thomson, Glasgow Road, was charged with creating a nuisance by keeping three young pigs. Mr Weir, sanitary inspector, said the neighbours complained, and on his making a search of the house, she endeavoured to hide the little ones, but latterly said she had only taken them in out of the cold, and it was so cruel to take her before the court. A fine of 10s was imposed.

WEEKLY RECORD   20TH JANUARY 1900

At Rutherglen Police Court, before Provost Kirkwood, Mrs Hunter, Glasgow Road, was fined 10s for harbouring young pigs in her dwelling house, situated two stairs up in a thickly populated tenement.

SOUTH SUBURBAN PRESS   27TH APRIL 1900

At the Queens Park Police Court — Bailie Oatts on the bench — Cosmo Capaldi, occupying premises at 381 Victoria Road and as such having a right to see the close or entry contigious to the premises and situated at 385 Victoria Road, was charged with having on the 31st March and on the 4th April, failed to sweep and wash the close in his turn. He pled guilty and was discharged with an admonition.

A boy of nine, named William Henderson, belonging to Annbank, pleaded guilty, before Sheriff Paterson at Ayr on Tuesday, to throwing a stone at the engine of a passing passenger train. In answer to the Sheriff the boys father undertook to give him 'a sound thrashing' and he was further ordered to leave £1 security for his good behaviour for six months.

At Campbeltown on Tuesday a large batch of defaulting parents were, at the instance of the Burgh School Board, fined in various amounts. One father was advised to tie his boy, a truant, to the bed at night and take him to school in the morning.

At the Edinburgh Burgh Court on Tuesday — Bailie Forbes MacKay on the bench — James Gibb, fruiterer, 93 Nicolson Street, was charged with contravening the shop Hours Act in having, during the week end Saturday 7th September, caused his assistant under 18 years of age, to be employed for a longer period than seventy four hours. The assistant was employed for 84 hours. The accused pleaded guilty and was fined 25s including expenses.

At the Queens Park Police Court on Friday — Bailie Dallas on the bench — George Sellars was charged with being drunk and incapable while in charge of a horse yoked to a cab in Pollockshaws Road the previous night. He pleaded not guilty. Two policemen gave evidence to the effect that while accused was able to stand he was too drunk to be in charge of a horse and cab in the public streets. The horse was going all over the street and in danger of coming in contact with other traffic. The charge was found proven and the Magistrate, in imposing a penalty of 10s 6d or 8 days, said it was a serious matter for the accused as well as the public and this could not be allowed.

PARTICK & MARYHILL PRESS   *5TH JULY 1907*

The Chief Constable called forward Constable Samuel Knox, whom he presented before Bailie A.M. Johnston, the presiding Magistrate stating that he had on 25th June apprehended two men in Minard Road in whose possession were found some lead piping and a number of brass taps which had been stolen from a wash house at 21 Hayburn Crescent by housebreaking.

Bailie Johnston complimented Constable Knox on his conduct on this occasion and presented him with a certificate and with a reward of 10s 6d, expressing the hope that he would continue to act as he had in the past, and that he would abstain from bad company and from strong drink.

GOVAN PRESS   *19TH JANUARY 1940*

William Longmuir (24), 65 Orchard Park Avenue, Giffnock, was sentenced to thirty days imprisonment at Glasgow Sheriff Court on Wednesday as the result of stealing 104 public library books, valued at £38 5s 6d relating to chemistry and kindred subjects.

GOVAN PRESS   *18TH APRIL 1941*

A fire watcher pleaded guilty to allowing a chimney of his house to catch fire while he was out on duty was fined 5s at the Southern Police Court on Tuesday. The accused stated: 'I left my wife to look after things as I was out fire watching on business premises.'

EVENING NEWS   *25TH JANUARY 1955*

In a Glasgow court case yesterday one of the witnesses gave evidence in the voice of the West Highlands. A succeeding witness made reference to him as 'the man that spoke wi' a foreign accent'.

GLASGOW HERALD   *12TH MARCH 1970*

A Glasgow man who needed 51 stitches to injuries he received after a lavatory pan gave way beneath him was yesterday awarded damages of £412 at Glasgow Sheriff Court. Mr. Gordon McLeod, Thornliebank, went to Kinning Park Public Baths in December, 1967, changed into swimming trunks and entered a toilet cubicle. He later emerged with cuts to his buttocks.

He sued Glasgow Corporation, owners of the baths, for loss of wages, shock, pain and discomfort.

Sheriff S.E. Bell, in his judgement said: 'I think the probabilities are that McLeod sat down more heavily than usual while slightly affected by drink, and fell to the bottom of the pan when it collapsed. It is pretty obvious there must have been a defect in the pan.' Mr McLeod said after hearing of the award: 'I had difficulty in sitting down for a number of months, but everything is back to normal now. I intend to buy my wife a new washing machine with the money.'

GLASGOW HERALD   *28TH JANUARY 1972*

Mr Charles Docherty, procurator fiscal depute, said at Glasgow Sheriff Court yesterday that when police officers spoke to a mynah bird in a house in Possilpark, Glasgow, on Wednesday night 'there was little or no reply from the bird'. But when the daughter of the owner of a pet shop in Maryhill, from which a mynah bird was stolen a week before, spoke to the bird 'lo and behold the bird spoke back'.

Charles Allison (17), Possilpark, pled guilty to the theft of the bird from the pet shop at 456 Maryhill Road on January 19th. Sheriff C.H. Johnstone Q.C. ordered reports on Allison, and remanded him in custody until February 16th.

EVENING CITIZEN   *6TH JULY 1972*

A man who tattooed the arm of a 15-year-old boy was fined £5 at Dunfermline Sheriff Court today. James Johnstone (34) unemployed labourer admitted the offence in his home on February 12th. The Fiscal said the boy in question had gone to Johnstone's home with an older youth. Johnstone had no sign in

the room pointing out it was illegal to tattoo someone under 18.

RUTHERGLEN REFORMER   14TH FEBRUARY 1974

When a police van was involved in a collision and
overturned a man stole the flashing beacon which
had become detached from the vehicle and at
Cambuslang J.P. Court last Thursday, William
McLachlan was fined £2 after pleading guilty to a
charge of stealing the blue light from the police van.
When he was cautioned and charged he replied: 'I
only wanted it as a souvenir.'

GLASGOW HERALD   9TH JANUARY 1979

A Stirling University student who was seen late one
night streaking along on a bicycle to win a £50 wager
from a friend was fined £50 at Stirling Sheriff Court.
Kenneth Marshall, Dunblane, admitted having rid-
den the cycle with no clothing on the lower part of
his body.

Depute Fiscal Mr Fergus Brown said that when
the police arrived Marshall streaked along the road
pursued by the officers, fell off his bike and cracked
his head on a gate.

The Chestnuts

GLASGOW ARGUS   *26TH SEPTEMBER 1836*

Two Irishmen were charged with fighting in Bridgegate. They denied it stoutly, one of them said his comrade at the bar was 'a little dafe, and he was only spakin' loud to let him hear — that was all — there was no fighting whatsomdever'. It was clearly proved, however, that there was not only 'loud Spakin' but that a good battle had been fought between the parties, and that too in the presence of a large crowd. The combatants were fined in 5s each.

GLASGOW SATURDAY POST   *22ND JUNE 1844*

On Friday in the Police Court, a hawker was fined in ten shillings for breaking a window and being always drunk. The prisoner denied the fact. He confessed he was drunk every day, but never on Sunday; and the officers acknowledged that was the truth.

GLASGOW EXAMINER   *9TH MARCH 1861*

On Friday morning last, a flesher from a neighbouring village, who had been cited to give evidence in a small debt case, made his appearance before Sheriff Barclay in such a state of intoxication as to render it utterly impossible to take his evidence. The case being concluded his Lordship found the witness guilty of contempt of court, and condemned him to pay a fine of ten shillings or go to prison for three days. While the clerk was reading over his decision the witness had to be supported in the box; but notwithstanding this, he persisted that he was 'as sober as a Judge'.

GLASGOW WEEKLY MAIL   *14TH FEBRUARY 1885*

At the Sheriff summary court on Monday — Sheriff Rutherford presiding — Georgina Madden, a middle aged woman, was charged with stealing a lady's jacket from the door of a draper's shop in West Nielson Street on Friday last. She pleaded guilty, saying she was so much the worse of drink as not to know what she was doing, that 'the thing flew past her with the wind, and she just caught it. She did not intend to steal it'. The Sheriff then passed sentence of 30 days imprisonment upon the prisoner against whom two previous convictions for theft were libelled.

WISHAW PRESS & ADVERTISER   *7TH MARCH 1885*

A labourer named Wm Allan, residing in Hope Street, Newmains admitted having staggered along Main Street on Sunday last whilst intoxicated. Prisoner said that on Saturday he had been to Glasgow to get a pair of boots and when arrested he was on the road home, he was tired with walking which probably made him stagger. He was fined 15s or 8 days imprisonment.

MOTHERWELL TIMES   *10TH APRIL 1886*

John had been out for a walk on Sunday but be could not enjoy it somehow. He could not at first understand how he was continually being dragged into the gutter and then against the wall. He made desperate efforts to walk straight but failed. Glancing down at his 'beetle crushers' he discovered the cause of his annoyance — he had put his boots on the wrong feet. No one could walk straight anymore than John with their boots transposed. Hardly fair John to fine you 5s or three days for making this small mistake.

GLASGOW WEEKLY MAIL   *21ST AUGUST 1886*

CAMPBELTOWN — Neil McLean and Neil McMillan, fishermen, were on Monday — before Bailie Muir — sent 30 days to prison for stealing porter out of a cask at the quay. The prisoners admitted the charge, and on being asked if they had anything to say for themselves, McLean, who has been before the Court recently for a similar offence, coolly asked the Magistrate if he would not take steps to prevent people laying temptation in the way of folk like him by putting casks on the quay with whisky and porter. It was too bad that it was allowed, and it was not easy for people like him to resist the temptation. The Bailie remarked that McLean had the matter in his own hands. Let him avoid the casks for the future.

GLASGOW WEEKLY MAIL   *23RD FEBRUARY 1889*

GREENOCK — At the Police Court on Saturday, George Mulherron was sent ten days to prison for stealing 21 eggs from a shed on the Custom-House Quay. The accused, in extenuation of the offence, said that he had taken the eggs, and had gone away with them. Something, however, told him that it was wrong, and he returned, and was in the act of replacing them when the policemen came up.

SOUTH SUBURBAN PRESS   *9TH MARCH 1889*

A respectable looking lad, residing in South York Street, was brought before Bailie Strong at Govanhill Police Court last Monday charged with stealing two bottles of beer from a basket on the footpath in Victoria Road. He pled guilty to the charge as read but when asked if he had to say anything on his behalf he replied: 'He thacht it was ginger'. This was his first offence, and after being detained some hours longer in custody he was allowed to go.

RUTHERGLEN REFORMER   *13TH NOVEMBER 1891*

John Johnston, piglifter, Porters Row, Gartsherrie, pleaded guilty of assaulting Thomas Dalziel and knocking him down on two occasions. He declared: 'If I hadn't struck him he would have struck me.' It struck the Magistrate, however, that Johnston should be fined 10s or seven days.

GLASGOW WEEKLY HERALD   *2ND JANUARY 1892*

Arthur William Crawford, who is said to have been a cowboy in Buffalo Bill's Wild West Troupe, was going along Duke Street on Friday, somewhat the worse for liquor.

He saw his reflection in a large mirror in a shop window, and thinking it was a man who contemplated an attack on him Crawford put up his fists, charged at his phantom opponent, breaking the window of the shop, and smashing the mirror. He was brought before Bailie Guthrie at the Eastern Police Court Monday, but was dismissed with an admonition. Crawford had a ticket for London in his possession and said he was going 'right there today'.

GLASGOW WEEKLY MAIL   *9TH APRIL 1892*

IRVINE — At the J.P. Court on Monday, Archibald Black, Captain of the yacht Maloom, was fined 10s for assaulting Charles Bird, steward on board the yacht. The Captain had been so annoyed by the snoring of Bird that for three nights he could not get sleeping, and at last determined to stop it, so he went to where Bird was sleeping and struck him a blow on the right eye, which not only stopped the snoring but wakened Bird. He appeared in Court with his discoloured eye.

WISHAW PRESS   *9TH JULY 1892*

Robert Templeton, mason, Muir Street, Hamilton, was charged with staggering under the influence of liquor in Glasgow Road on Sunday and pleaded not guilty The police evidence was to the effect that the accused was 'taking the breadth of the road' and smelt of liquor. Templeton said that it was corns on his feet that caused his staggering. The Court refused to accept this excuse and imposed a penalty of 10s or 7 days imprisonment.

AIRDRIE ADVERTISER   *1ST JULY 1893*

John Stewart, a boy, was charged with breaking some window glass in a house in Lugar Street by throwing stones. It was explained that he was aiming a stone at a hole in the window when it struck a whole pane. The lad was fined 1s and cautioned.

WISHAW PRESS   *24TH MARCH 1894*

John Boyle, miner, Thomson Square, Law pleaded guilty to being drunk and incapable in Main Street on the previous day. He was sentenced to pay 3 half crowns or go five days to jail. Boyle who is not unfamiliar with Court etiquette, seemed delighted that the punishment was not heavier.

The Bailie: 'But you must bear in mind that if you come up here again the fine will not be 7s 6d.'

Accused: 'I won't come up if they don't fetch me.'

Rutherglen Reformer   *7th June 1895*

John Smith, miner, 17 North Nimmos Lane, for a breach of the peace on Friday last, was fined 5s or 3 days. One of the witnesses remarked, when asked by the Fiscal if accused was worse of drink, that he was and she thought 'they were making it extra strong now'. *(laughter)*

Glasgow Weekly Mail   *1st June 1895*

John Kelly was a brawny Irishman. He wore boots that a diver would have envied. John was accused of adding a shirt to his wardrobe without paying.

Agnes McCormich: 'I am a girl in Mr Robert Miller's shop at 15 Gallowgate. There were four shirts hanging out at the door. I noticed one was away, and that the rest were lying in the street. I saw a man with something bulky under his arm walk quickly away. I told a policeman and he apprehended the man. The shirt was discovered under his coat.'

Kelly: 'Where any shirt ought to be.'

Mrs Walker: 'I saw the prisoner and two others come up against the shop door. Indeed, they knocked up against me. I saw one of the men shove the shirt under his oxter.'

Kelly: 'Now, yer 'onner the thing is this. The man jhust put the shirt under me arm.'

Magistrate: 'You should have thrown it down and said you did not wish a shirt that way. Fifteen days.'

SOUTH SUBURBAN PRESS   8TH FEBRUARY 1896

A female vagrant named Helen Johnston, before Bailie John Murray at Queens Park on Friday on a charge of having been found drunk and incapable in Cathcart Road on the previous day. 'My Lord', she said with a profound courtesy, 'Oi took a little dhrop of dhrink, a' was travellin', my Lord, with little bits o' things. Oi was goin' to moi friends in the 'eilans tomorrow my Lord', and she produced a line. At which the Prosecutor smiled, for the story was what is vulgarly known as a chestnut. He said he had known Helen for ten years, she had been a regular customer at the Central, and she had always the same story. Her 'friends in the 'eilans' seemed always to be sending for her just as she got into trouble. 'People hawking', quoth the Bailie, 'should not take drink', whereupon Helen said she had not taken it for two years until she was badly on Thursday. The Bailie: '10s 6d or seven days in prison' and Helen left the court pronouncing her worst curses on all and sundry — all, according to her enlightenment, being the biggest blackguards between a certain warm region and her home in Connaught.

MOTHERWELL TIMES   5TH JULY 1895

Thomas Thomson, shoemaker, Quarry Street, Hamilton pleaded guilty to indecently exposing himself in Union and Leslie Streets on Saturday. In extenuation the accused explained that he was so drunk he did not know what he was doing and took his clothes off thinking he was going to bed. He was fined 5s or three days.

PARKHEAD, BRIDGETON, SHETTLESTON
& TOLLCROSS ADVERTISER   *31ST MARCH 1896*

At the Eastern Police Court, on Friday morning Joseph Jamison was fined three guineas, or 30 days imprisonment, for having in Canning Street, Calton, made a savage and unprovoked attack on a policeman. The Constable had been engaged in what is known in the force as 'passing an order', and whistled to his neighbour on the neighbouring beat. Jamison passing at the time evidently was under some misapprehension as to this action, and exclaiming, 'Do you want to take Jamison up again?' set upon the unoffending policeman and severely maltreated him.

WISHAW PRESS   *14TH APRIL 1896*

Mary Malley or McGarry, Sunnyside Rows was accused of being drunk and incapable in Caledonian Road on Saturday 7th inst.

The Bailie: 'Are you guilty Mary?'

Accused: 'Your honour, the trimming of my frock tripped me, and I was not able to rise.'

The Assessor: 'It was an accident then?'

Accused: 'Oh no, I admit I had a glass or two.'

The Assessor: 'Then it was the whisky that tripped you?'

A penalty of 10s or seven days imprisonment having been imposed. Mary remarked 'I think that's rather much, your honour, I didn't make enough noise for 10s.'

SOUTH SUBURBAN PRESS   *12TH JUNE 1896*

William Curran an Albert Street youth was charged with having early on Sunday morning last, assaulted a labourer in a close at 89 Albert Street, by striking him and otherwise creating a breach of the peace. Accused pled guilty and said he did it in 'fence deself'. *(laughter)*

Fiscal: 'You mean "self-defence"?'

Accused: 'Yes.'

Bailie: 'Ten and sixpence or seven days.'

GLASGOW WEEKLY MAIL   *17TH OCTOBER 1896*

At Queens Park Police Court on Wednesday — Bailie Alexanderton on the bench, James Blair, labourer, was fined 21s with the option of 14 days in jail, for having assaulted a twelve year old boy on Saturday night. The accused, it seemed, had seen the boy playing with others on the pavement in Aitkenhead Road, Govanhill, and had lifted him and thrown him at a plate glass window — in a joke, he said — both window and boy were damaged.

GOVAN PRESS   *26TH OCTOBER 1896*

The last prisoner called at Plantation Police Court on Monday was Jane Christie or Marshall and the charge against her was that she had been drunk and incapable on Saturday morning. She said she had never been drunk in her life. A policeman went into the witness box and related how he came across accused in a state of intoxication.

Fiscal: 'Do you hear that?'

Accused: 'Is that me? That'll no dae Maister.'

Fiscal: 'Was it not you then?'

Accused: 'I don't know.'

Fiscal: 'Who brought you here?'

Accused: 'I hae a bad memory and the doctor put seven yairds o' flannel round ma heid and I canny tell you the day in th' week.'

The woman was allowed to go.

GOVAN PRESS   *22ND JULY 1898*

At Govan Police Court on Tuesday — Bailie Smith on the bench — an aged woman named Elizabeth Armstrong or Donnelly was presented to answer to a charge of having assaulted Matilda Donnelly or Dunlop in Victoria Street the previous afternoon.

The Magistrate: 'Did you strike the woman?'

Lizzie: 'Sure I never struck tae woman at all, it was the whisky inside me that did it.'

The Magistrate remarked that it was very convenient at this time of the year to blame everything on the whisky. He would let her off with seven and sixpence. Accused on leaving the bar, observed, amid laughter, 'With seven and sixpence Bailie Smith, you must pay 7s 6d or in default undergo 5 days imprisonment.'

WEEKLY RECORD   *17TH MARCH 1900*

At the Justice of Peace Court, Irvine, on Monday, Walter Sneddon, miner, Kilwinning, was fined 10s for having failed to provide necessary education for his child. The accused looked surprised and said: 'My boy is 13 years and 6 months. He is over 10 stone and fit to marry.'

SPRINGBURN ADVERTISER   8TH MARCH 1900

An elderly woman appeared at St Rollox Police Court on Saturday charged with being intoxicated in a lobby in Townhead with two children under her care. Police evidence having been given, accused said 'I wis oot a message to Garscube Road, an', as I'm awfu' bothered with toothache, I took a wee hauf.' *(laughter)*

Bailie Oatts: 'And did the toothache make you drunk?'

Accused: 'Naw; I doot it wis the dram I took, I'm awfu' easy knockit up.'

Bailie: 'Toothache is a bad thing in itself, but the cure you took is worse. Have you ever been in trouble before?'

Accused: 'Naw your honour, sir.'

Bailie: 'Well, you can go this morning.'

Accused: 'Thank you kindly Bailie, thank you kindly.'

SPRINGBURN ADVERTISER   17TH MAY 1900

David Calderwood, middle aged, with red face and unkempt beard, caused some amusement in St Rollox Police Court on Monday. He was charged with having on Saturday night, in Garngad·Road, used bad language — an accusation which he emphatically denied. A constable stepped into the witness box and gave evidence against the prisoner. David, looking at the policeman with an aggrieved air said 'I thought you only brought me here for a joke', adding musingly and as if struck with an afterthought, 'If

I'd stood ye a drink it would have been all right. Aye and many a one I've stood ye.'

Bailie to Constable: 'Did he ever stand you any drink?'

Constable: 'No your honour.'

Bailie: 'I find the charge proved. Seven and six or ten days.'

David threw a scornful look at the bench, and sauntered off to the cells.

Wishaw Press   *31st March 1900*

A miner named Adam Powell residing at Meadowhill Road, Larkhall, tendered a plea of guilty to a charge of using obscene language on Saturday 24th inst. in a posting yard in Wishaw. He explained that he was lying asleep in a brake awaiting his companions, who returned while he slept and set fire to his moustache, which, he said was a heavy one, the result being the complete destruction of his hirsute adornment, while he suffered no little pain from the effects of the burning. He was mulcted in a penalty of 20s or fourteen days imprisonment.

Weekly Record   *17th November 1900*

A man named, Wm James Donnelly, who was charged at Greenock Police Court on Tuesday with the theft of a handbag from a shop-door in West Blackhall Street, stated that fifteen years ago he was bitten by a dog, and since then had been inclined to thieving. He did not know whether the dog had poisoned his blood or not, nor did he know how the bag came to be in his possession. He was sent to prison for 20 days.

SPRINGBURN ADVERTISER   14TH AUGUST 1902

Mary Briton or Coyle stood laughing at the bar of St Rollox Police Court on Monday morning, when she was charged with maliciously breaking 12 panes of glass in the window of the house of Elizabeth Findley, at 51 Castle Street. When asked for her reason for doing this Mary again burst into laughter, and stated she did it in self defence. The Bailie passed sentence of 5s or three days.

SPRINGBURN ADVERTISER   4TH AUGUST 1904

A woman named Catherine Docherty or Buchanan, arrived at Barnhill Poorhouse, on Thursday night, and was taken inside. While there, however, she failed to conform to the necessary regulations, and caused a disturbance, with the result that she had to be given in charge of the police.

At the Court she denied the charge, and evidence was led as to her conduct. Addressing the prisoner Judge J.H. Martin asked if she had any witnesses.

Accused: 'God, is my only witness.'

Magistrate: 'Well, we can't put Him in the box. 14 days imprisonment.'

POLLOCKSHAWS NEWS   13TH DECEMBER 1907

Thomas McQuilter, quarryman, 44 Pleasance Street, pleaded guilty to a charge of being drunk. He said that he had sore teeth, and took four glasses of rum on an empty stomach to deaden the pain. He was fined 7s 6d or imprisonment for five days.

RUTHERGLEN REFORMER   5TH APRIL 1963

Glasgow motorist Edward Airlie will be arrested this month and jailed for a lighting offence. He told Rutherglen Police Court that he would not pay the fine imposed by Bailie Andrew Moffat for parking his car on a street without lights. Mr Airlie (34), sales manager, explained that he had left his lights on and that the battery had run flat.

When Bailie Moffat announced a fine, Mr Airlie asked: 'What was the option?'

Bailie: 'Twenty days imprisonment?'

Mr Airlie: 'I'll take it.'

But the court refused. 'You have 14 days to pay', John Hill the clerk said to him.

Later Mr Airlie said he was determined to go to prison when the 14 days expired.

EVENING CITIZEN   *6TH JULY 1972*

Found smoking a cannabis cigarette in the toilet of a public house a 22 year old man told the police: 'You are right, man...it's a joint.'

At Hamilton Sheriff court today John McCumisky, London, admitted having had a quantity of cannabis, Sheriff Ian Dickson fined him £100.

RUTHERGLEN REFORMER   *26TH JUNE 1974*

A youth cautioned at Rutherglen Police Station for making a 'Harvey Smith' sign at a passing patrol car couldn't take a telling, and minutes after being released landed back in the station for committing a similar offence. The court heard that John Simmons of Toryglen, Rutherglen, was taken to the police station on May 3rd for making a rude gesture at a passing police car. Minutes after being freed Simmons was back inside the station for committing a similar offence. He was fined £10.

Sheriff Ewan Stewart put a price on honesty yesterday at Wick Sheriff Court. Given £100,000 he said he would take a gamble on crime. Sheriff Stewart was dealing with a case of pilfering, he told Donald McIntosh Sutherland that the articles he had stolen from his employer were just not worth the risk. He was fined £25.

The Sheriff told McIntosh everyone was tempted in a moment's loose thinking to steal and he reckoned £100,000 would be a generally acceptable return for running the risk of discovery and its consequences.

The Sheriff added: 'Offer me that amount and I am your man. I am willing to take a chance on that, but not for less.'

A woman whose husband suffered from agoraphobia and could not leave the house to work, but who could go out drinking has been divorced. Mrs Agnes Readie, Govanhill, Glasgow, was granted decree of divorce by Lord Leissen in the Court of Session yesterday on the grounds of the cruelty of her husband Charles Readie. The issue in the case was whether his conduct was sufficiently grave to constitute cruelty, the Judge said he had no doubt it did.

A Bathgate man complained about the room service and being awakened at six in the morning... when he was in a police cell. The joke misfired and ended with an assault of Constable John McAuley, Linlithgow Sheriff Court was told today. John O'Hara (51) Bathgate, was fined £100 for the assault and for a breach of the peace in Armadale.

GLASGOW HERALD   23RD JANUARY 1979

A court had to be convened in a police cell in Aberdeen yesterday after a prisoner took all his clothes off and refused to appear at the Sheriff Court. William Dalziel Smith (35), Aberdeen, faced Sheriff Peter Hamilton, court officials and police wearing only handcuffs and a blanket. He denied stealing a ring, committing a breach of the peace and assaulting a woman in an Aberdeen lounge bar and was remanded in custody for trial on February 9th.

A court official said later: 'It is very unusual for a Sheriff to reconvene a court in the police cells.'

EVENING TIMES   27TH JANUARY 1984

A teenager was ordered not to sniff glue or solvents. Charles Boswell (19) was told he would be guilty of an offence under the Bail (Scotland) Act if he did, and that could land him behind bars. The move by Sheriff Shiach came after an amazing outburst by Boswell at Linlithgow Sheriff Court, West Lothian. After the Sheriff told him he was considering community service Boswell interjected: 'Could you not make my community service on a Saturday, because that's the day I sniff glue.' Boswell, had a sentence deferred on a charge of breaking into a primary school with intent to steal.

The Amazons

GLASGOW ARGUS   *30TH APRIL 1838*

Helan Machon, was convicted of theft, aggravated by being habit and repute a thief and having previous convictions. The prisoner, during her trial, upbraided some of the witnesses as being thieves themselves, and on hearing her sentence, seven years transportation, she assured the court that she would make an effort to get a black man in the country to which she should be sent.

SATURDAY POST   *30TH MARCH 1844*

At the bar of the Gorbals Police Court, on Wednesday, a notorious street walker and pest, being convicted and ordered to be sent to Bridewell by the sitting Bailie, lifted a piece of coal, which she managed to conceal beneath her apron and let fly at his worship's head. Fortunately, however the Bailie noticed the prisoner's movement in time, and ducked his head, otherwise he might have been knocked down by the missile.

GLASGOW GLASGOW SENTINEL   *26TH FEBRUARY 1870*

At Greenock Police Court on Monday before Bailie W Neill, the notorious Christina McTaggart was again placed at the bar, charged with having committed a breach of the peace in Cathcart Square on Sunday morning, and was sent to jail for 60 days. Christina, who is only a few days out of prison, when placed at the bar on Monday behaved in the most unbecoming manner. On the number of her convictions being intimated, she told the Fiscal that if he minded his prayers as well as he appeared to mind the number of convictions recorded against her it would be a good thing for him. Her subsequent bad language was very reprehensible.

GLASGOW SENTINEL   5TH MAY 1877

A burly looking female of unmistakable Celtic origin was recently arraigned before the Magistrate for some ordinary offence. While nature had magnificently endowed her with good health and physical strength, the question of good looks had been neglected in the haste in which she had been prepared for the world.

'What are you up here for?' inquired the Magistrate.

'My beauty, I reckon.'

'Your what?'

'My beauty.'

'Are you certain of that?'

'Oh bedad, aye there's no mistake.'

'Then I discharge you — you ain't guilty.'

And the acquitted lady took her departure.

RUTHERGLEN REFORMER   28TH JULY 1877

Mary Hannah or Early and Mary McDonald or Cummerford were sent 30 days to prison for giving too much liberty to their tongues. Even in court they could not be restrained from giving 'his honour' a taste of their quality.

GLASGOW WEEKLY MAIL   23RD APRIL 1887

ALLOA — On Monday, at the Police Court — Bailie McDowall on the bench — Mary Jardine or Manion, wife of a labourer, residing in Broad Street, was convicted of molesting the police, and was fined 10s or seven days in prison. The evidence showed that the woman, who is not unknown to the police, on Saturday night after 11 o'clock, made a complaint to the constables that three men were making a disturbance by kicking at her door.

On the two officers entering the house to make inquiries of her husband, Mary coolly left the house, locking the street door behind her, leaving the policemen prisoners, at the same time telling the crowd outside how she had 'tricked' the police. In about a quarter of an hour, the accused returned and relieved her prisoners amidst the laughter of a large crowd.

RUTHERGLEN REFORMER   *6TH MAY 1887*

Bridget Shale, described as a spinster, residing in Langloan, was charged with being found drunk and incapable, the Superintendent stating that she had been in an awful state, and taken to the office in a wheelbarrow, Bridget was fined half crown.

AIRDRIE ADVERTISER   *4TH FEBRUARY 1888*

On Monday, Ann Leonard or Mallon (54) an old offender, wife of a collier at Arden Rows, was brought before ex-Provost Black and Mr Andrew Aitken in the J.P. Court, and convicted of a charge of assault and breach of the peace. She had gone into the store at Arden and created a disturbance, in the course of which she attacked and greatly interrupted a lad named John Cowan, the storeman who was serving customers. Among other things, she threw a quart of beer in his face and shied some turnips at him over the counter. She was sentenced to 9 days imprisonment, on hearing which she exclaimed 'Ten years! Eh, ye've done for me noo!' *(laughter)*

GOVAN PRESS   *8TH DECEMBER 1888*

Mary McMahon a young woman with no fixed residence was charged with breach of the peace in Knowe Street early on Tuesday morning. It appeared from her father's statement, who appeared in court, that the prisoner had left her home, and was in the habit of annoying her parents and the neighbours at unreasonable hours. She was sent to prison for ten days without the option of a fine. When being led out she cried, 'I can do that lot on my head!'

9th August 1889

Agnes Gribben pled guilty to assaulting a man whom she alleged kicked her. The Fiscal caused the court to laugh by informing it that this was a physical impossibility, as the man had only one leg. She had only come out of prison on Saturday. She was sent to gaol for twenty days

Pollockshaws News *16th May 1890*

Agnes Gribben, Shawhill Street, pled guilty to assaulting Annie White in a house in Shawhill Street, and afterwards committing a breach of the peace. Agnes always pleads guilty, but reminds the court, that she is not guilty and only sacrifices herself to save other people trouble. For her sacrifice this time she was ordered to pay 7s 6d or go to prison for four days.

Wishaw Press *22nd November 1890*

Theressa McEwan or McDonald, an elderly woman with no fixed residence, pleaded guilty to a charge of being drunk and incapable in Main Street on Saturday night.

The Fiscal (to the prisoner): 'What is your occupation? I heard you were an actress.'

Prisoner: 'An actress? Oh no, if I said that, I must have been raving with the drink'.

The accused was fined 5s or 24 hours imprisonment.

Esther Edith or Bell was a poor-looking dirty woman as she stood up and pleaded not guilty to a charge of throwing stones and altogether behaving in a disorderly manner near the Clifton Iron Works. She was described as the wife of a labourer, residing in Kirkintilloch but was now living apart from her husband. She appears to have suffered most herself by her stone throwing, as one of them came down and struck her on the head, but that was not to be the end of her woes for 20s or fourteen days was clapped on her to crown all.

Provost Maclean was in a lenient mood on Monday, and was inclined to be merciful. At the Plantation Police Court a woman named Jane Graham or Fraser, a widow, pleaded guilty to being drunk and incapable on Saturday night. The Provost said he would give her a chance and let her go if she promised not to take whisky anymore. Jane readily consented and left the bar. A few minutes afterwards she was discovered along with a female friend going into a 'pub' in the neighbourhood evidently determined on giving practical effect to her promise to the Chief Magistrate of Govan.

Mary Proctor or Lawlar was charged with cursing while on an outside stairlanding in Walker Street on Saturday.

Bailie: 'Are you guilty?'

The accused looked bewildered. 'A ken naething aboot it. I was tin my bed when I heard a noise and cam oot tae see whit it wis, when the police jist took me.'

Constable Sutherland said she had a great crowd of people gathered about. She was making a great noise and using very bad language.

Bailie: 'Who was she swearing at?'

Constable: 'Her own man. He cannot put up with her, and is going to leave her.'

Bailie: 'Well I think her man and her will better separate for a while. A guinea or 30 days.'

GLASGOW WEEKLY MAIL   15TH APRIL 1893

On Wednesday Thomas Burns, whose eccentric behaviour excited a deal of attention, was placed at the bar of the City Police Court charged with creating a distrubance by shouting and swearing in Parliament Square on Monday. The accused pleaded strongly with the Magistrate to let him off.

'No' replied the Bailie, 'I will give you ten days.'

'Ten days', exclaimed the prisoner as he was removed to the cells, 'Oh, my poor feet!'

Agnes McMurray or Elliot, widow, Main Street, pleaded guilty to a charge of creating a breach of the peace, by using abusive language to another woman. Mr Ramsey, who imposed a sentence of 10s or seven days, said he had some sympathy with Agnes, for he thought a woman's tongue was always beyond control; but women were responsible for the offences of their tongue, and she would have to suffer.

A voice: 'Thank God'. *(laughter)*

Agnes: 'I've paid weel for my cairry-on.'

Agnes had a great deal to say as she was leaving the Court and Mr Ramsey had to caution her to draw it mild.

Jane Ferguson, a young woman, who has been frequently before the Court, and who gained some notoriety a year or two ago by throwing a scone at the head of Stipendiary Gemmel, was again before the Central Police Court on Saturday. The charge was one of disorderly conduct. She entered the Court carrying one of her boots in her right hand, and as a precautionary measure it was deemed advisable to hold her while she stood at the bar. Thus restrained from actual violence she made free use of her tongue, cursed and swore, and conducted herself in a very obstreperous manner. Bailie Martin who occupied the bench sentenced her to 60 days imprisonment.

GOVAN PRESS   29TH JULY 1893

Mrs McDonald, an elderly woman, ill-clad and decidedly haggard looking, came before Provost Kirkwood and Bailie Carmichael at Govan Police Court on Wednesday and to a charge of assaulting a widow, and using abusive language in McLean Street on the 25th inst pleaded that she was 'Guilty so far'.

'And how far may that be?' genially inquired the Provost.

'Well I dinna think I struck her', replied the accused, 'but really I dinna ken what I dune.'

Ultimately pleading guilty, a penalty of 10s 6d or seven days was imposed.

GOVAN PRESS   4TH AUGUST 1894

Bridget Sweeny or Grimes of familiar face at Albert Street was charged at Govan Police Court on Monday with having assaulted a labourer in Hamilton Street on Saturday, also with cursing and swearing in Breach of the Peace. She pleaded not guilty and produced a handful of hair which, she alleged, was torn from her head by a witness.

The first witness stated that he was going up the stairs when the accused rushed out and struck him and began to curse and swear. She was worse for drink. The next witness, Mrs McDonald, on being asked her name said 'You should ken it by heart now, I'm here often enought.'

Accused (to witness after evidence): 'A glass of whisky could buy you any day.'

Witness: 'I wish I had one just now to put the shakers off me.'

Fiscal: 'Have you any witnesses?'

Accused: 'Yes, I've one, but she's not here'.

Magistrate: 'You are here too often, you don't expect I will pass you this time. If you can't agree with your neighbours you should leave. Fifteen shillings or ten days.'

GOVAN PRESS   *20TH JANUARY 1894*

There was a rehearsal of Shakespeare's plays in Govan last week but somehow the actresses had mistaken their parts. The scene was changed on Monday to the Albert Street Theatre where Margaret Warren or Koatings occupied a 'box' and was found guilty of having assaulted Mary Jane Munro or Crawford. The performance was not repeated, and whether as a recompense for disappointing the audience or not we cannot say, but the Judge ordered her to stump up 21s or go to the 'green room' for 14 days.

PARTICK STAR   *22ND SEPTEMBER 1894*

On Tuesday before Bailie Frew, Mary Ann McLean or Burns, having no fixed residence, was charged with committing a breach of the peace the previous day. She was very noisy in Court, and treated the Constables to some very unseemly language. She remonstrated strongly against being locked up, and remarked that 'the Queen knew her, for she had 'danced with her in a public house at Bridge-of-Weir'. The prisoner was then removed, it being considered that she was deranged.

Partick & Maryhill Press   *3rd November 1894*

Sarah Johnstone or McPherson pleaded not guilty to a charge of having assaulted a woman and committed a breach of peace. One of the witnesses made reference to her daughter-in-law.

Fiscal: 'Who's your daughter-in-law?'

Witness: 'My son's wife.' *(laughter)*

The case was found proven but accused was admonished.

Glasgow Weekly Mail   *2nd March 1895*

Catherine Mulloy or Monks was old. She had a chest complaint that made her sigh like a country undertaker. Although she had one foot in the grave, she had had the other in a public house. She was charged with cursing and swearing.

Catherine: 'Me, me?'

A young woman stepped into the box and said: 'That's my aunty.'

Catherine: 'I haven't spoken to her for two months, not since the last time we were in the coort.'

The Niece: 'She was drunk and cursing and swearing.'

Magistrate: '7s 6d or five days'.

Catherine: 'Oh my, my — my cough will be the waur o' this.'

Partick Star   *31st July 1895*

At the Plantation Police Court on Monday — Bailie McKerrow on the bench — Flora Stevenson or Bryson was fined 10s 6d or seven days in jail for having used obscene language on a stair in Cornwall Street. On hearing the sentence she remarked, 'That's all right, I can pay the 10s 6d.'

SOUTH SUBURBAN PRESS   *7TH DECEMBER 1895*

Margaret Stewart or Congleton, 15 Polmadie Street, who now needs no direction to the Queens Park Police Office, appeared before Bailie Thomson on Wednesday on a charge of having been riotous and disorderly in her behaviour on the stair leading to her house, on the 26th inst.

She pleaded guilty, and in reply to the Magistrate said she had nothing to say for herself, except that she had got among a bad lot of neighbours.

Mrs McQueen said the row had started by accused saying she would send 'the Sanitary' to her. She (witness) retorted that it was accused who needed 'the Sanitary' whereupon, accused also called one of my children 'rotton.'

The Assessor: 'Does she drink?'

Witness: 'Drink! She's never sober.' *(laughter)*

The Magistrate: 'Ten shillings and sixpence or fourteen days.'

PARTICK & MARYHILL PRESS   *28TH MARCH 1896*

Catherine Foley or Campbell, a diminutive little personage who might easily be attached to the end of a watch chain, as an appendage, was disorderly in Bridge Street on Saturday night and making noise enough for ten women thrice her size. She has 'been here before' and was fined 7s 6d or five days.

Partick & Maryhill Press   25th April 1896

Agnes Galt or Hector, residing at 4 Campbell Street, was charged with assaulting Elizabeth McKinnon or Kerr from the window of her house, by throwing a quantity of earth in her face. She was fined in 5s or 3 days. Although Agnes had in her possession a P.O. for £2 15s she refused to pay the fine, and by doing so had the whole of the 'Black Maria' to herself. Wednesday, by the way was a splendid day for carriage exercise.

Glasgow Weekly Mail   25th July 1896

GREENOCK — At Monday's Police Court, Rose Ann Gallacher made her 189th appearance, and was charged with drunkeness. Bailie Mitchell, who presided, asked 'What are we to do with you, you have been 115 times previously convicted for this same offence alone?' Accused offered no opinion and was fined in 21s or 14 days imprisonment.

South Suburban Press   13th February 1897

A stairhead quarrel between Margaret Dodds or Downie and Christian Sandison or Spence both residing at 11 MacLean Street culminated in a report to the police authorities on Saturday, when Mrs Spence charged Mrs Downie with breach of the peace and produced witnesses to swear that Mrs Downie called her 'a daft bitch' and said her daughter should put her in an asylum. The charge was found not proven.

GOVAN PRESS   *27TH FEBRUARY 1897*

Rosanne Ferguson pled guilty of breach of the peace, and abusive and obscene language (directed against no one in particular) in Paisley Road on Saturday night. She was fined 21s or fourteen days imprisonment.

GLASGOW EVENING NEWS   *29TH JANUARY 1898*

Annie McCraw, a respectably dressed young woman residing at 40 Dunmore Street, was placed at the bar of the Southern Police Court today, charged with the theft of her mother's set of false teeth. She admitted taking them out of the house in her pocket, but denied that she had any intention of stealing them.

The Bailie (to Mrs McCraw): 'What's the value of the teeth to her?'

Mrs McCraw: 'They are no use to her, yer Honour. She has got good teeth of her own.'

The case was dismissed.

PARTICK & MARYHILL PRESS   *22ND APRIL 1898*

Mary Logue or Lafferty, when her case was called at the Police Court on Monday replied with alacrity, 'I am here'. She stood up at the bar smiling at all and sundry. She was charged with having, on the 5th April, at 25 Newton Street, behaved in a disorderly manner by cursing and swearing, kicking at a door and pushing it open. Mary pleaded not guilty.

During the evidence Mary cross-examined with great volubility. In the midst of a torrent of irrelevant remarks addressed to the Magistrates and officials, the bar officer tried to intervene, on which accused said 'Keep your hands off me; I am a married woman!'

Provost Caird: 'We will need to find you guilty.'

Accused: 'All right, I got seven days for this on Holy Thursday.'

Provost Caird: 'What does your husband do?'

Accused: 'He is a plasterer's labourer, but he will not pay my fine.'

Provost Caird: 'I think he is quite right, he is anxious to get rid of you.'

Accused: 'Well I can't help it, it is just my nature.'

Provost Caird: '21s or 14 days.'

Accused: 'Very well.'

GLASGOW WEEKLY HERALD   *9TH JULY 1898*

On Monday morning, Maggie Stewart or Hendry, aged 26 years, wife of a sailor, gave birth to a female child in a cell in the Southern Police Office. The woman was taken into custody on a charge of disorderly conduct, and appeared at the Southern Police Court that morning, when she was fined 10s 6d, with the option of seven days imprisonment. The mother and baby are doing well.

PARTICK STAR   8TH APRIL 1899

Susan Redpath or Johnston, residing at 102 Douglas Street, made her 141st appearance at the Police Court on Wednesday on a charge of having created a disturbance in Dumbarton Road, on Tuesday night. She was sentenced to 60 days imprisonment.

SPRINGBURN ADVERTISER   7TH MAY 1903

A woman named Annie Ridge denied the charge of using obscene language in Glebe Street about a quarter past one on Sunday morning.

A Constable spoke to the language which accused was using. 'She was along with a man, he further added.

Prisoner: 'He is not a man; he 's my husband.'

The Bailie: 'Is your husband not a man? *(laughter)* 10s 6d or seven days.'

SPRINGBURN ADVERTISER   16TH JULY 1903

An Auchinarin woman, named Mary Ann MacDonald appeared at the St Rollox Police Court on Saturday morning, on a charge of being drunk the day previous.

The Bailie: 'Were you drunk?'

Prisoner: 'Aye, for years.' *(loud laughter)*

Bailie Mitchell admonished the old body.

POLLOCKSHAWS NEWS   3RD JUNE 1904

Martha Brown or Hendry, 54 Main Street, was guilty of a breach of the peace. She had got too much drink.

The Magistrate desired to know in which public house she was supplied with liquor, and her reply was that she had been in nearly all the public houses. Fined 10s or imprisonment for seven days.

POLLOCKSHAWS NEWS   *9TH FEBRUARY 1906*

A scene of an exciting and extraordinary character was witnessed in the Burgh Court on Monday forenoon. John Neil, labourer, 31 Pleasance Street, Mary McPhelim or Neil, his wife, and Jane Rutherford or Dougan, 8 Shawhill Street, were charged with creating a breach of the peace. Bailie McLellan found them all guilty and fined the man in 10s or seven days, the women being each fined in 5s or imprisonment for three days.

After being sentenced the women fell out and began to use language of the worst description to one another. They were ordered to desist, but they paid no attention to the command and in a minute or two came to blows. They were separated by the police after a violent struggle and removed from the court. Mrs Dougan calling on someone to hold her wean till she got at the other woman.

GOVAN PRESS   *11TH FEBRUARY 1944*

'Keep away from American soldiers for your own sake,' said Bailie Alice Cullen in admonishing a 19-year-old girl who appeared before the bar on a charge of creating a nuisance by singing and shouting outside premises at Paisley Road West.

'These premises,' said the Fiscal, 'are a rendez-vous for American soldiers and complaints have been received about the conduct of the young girls who frequent them.'

GOVAN PRESS   *27TH AUGUST 1954*

The police set a trap to catch street footballers in Hoey Street, but they were spoiled when a housewife Mrs Jenny Joyce shouted a warning. She was fined 10s at Govan Police Court last Friday. She ran through a close ahead of the police shouting 'L.O.P.!' and the footballers escaped. This is a warning cry in this area and means either 'Look out, police' or 'Lay off — polis', the Fiscal Mr W.A. Grindlay explained to the court.

GLASGOW HERALD   *6TH JUNE 1987*

A Glasgow fruitseller has won a battle against the council, and can now go to the toilet — thanks to a Sheriff's ruling. Mrs Helen McCluskie works 10 hours a day, six days a week at her busy stall in Argyle Street. She could not leave the stall, at the corner at Virginia Street from 8am until 6pm — not even to spend a penny. The district council refused to let her son Gerald stand in, and also refused to grant him a licence. The 23-year-old could not even carry the heavy crates of fruit and vegetables from the family van. Now he has been told he will get a street trading licence — by court order, Sheriff Ian Price overturned a decision by the licensing committee.

The Conmen

GLASGOW ARGUS   *9TH SEPTEMBER 1833*

A young fellow was apprehended on Saturday by the police, charged with a novel method of swindling the citizens out of their property. He has been in the habit of representing himself as a painter, and calling hastily at doors for the loan of a pair of steps or a chair, only for a few minutes, as he was in the habit of remarking, till he altered a sign, or a street number in the neighbourhood. Uniformly, when the article was got, he disappeared with it, and as uniformly, it was afterwards found at the door of some broker, to whom he had sold it. His malpractices in this way became exceedingly annoying, and he was not long ago confined in Bridewell on a charge of this description.

GLASGOW HERALD   *5TH JUNE 1837*

A person in the dress of a sailor, and pretending to be a native of France, and in a state of destitution, has been going about this city (Edinburgh) for some time past, imposing on the generosity of the citizens. He has, however, been captured by the police. One night's confinement has enabled him to speak English.

Glasgow Saturday Post   23rd April 1842

A well known chaindropper, named John McFadyen, was apprehended on Monday near the Broomielaw, attempting, in the practice of his vacation to swindle an Irishman out of some money, for a purse containing a chain and two seals, which the former pretended to find upon the pavement after he got into the company of the latter.

Poor Paddy, however, was just about to leave for Ireland, and all the money he had in his possession not amounting to the tithe of what he was expected to pay to his fortunate colleague, as his share of a prize which had been valued by a gentleman on the street, to whose judgement the matter had been referred, at £16, some delay was occasioned in bringing the matter to a conclusion, when a policeman, whose attention had been previously directed to the movements of McFadyen, stepped forward and took the vagabond into custody. The gentleman who had valued the articles, however got clear off. The intrinsic value of the purse and its contents is considered to be under half a crown. McFadyen was brought before the Police Court on Wednesday, when he was clearly convicted and sentenced to 30 days confinement in Bridewell.

Glasgow Saturday Post   23rd December 1843

At the Glasgow Police Court on Tuesday forenoon a young fellow, well known to the Police, was sent 60 days to Bridewell for stealing a bonnet off a man's head in one of the wynds. It appears that the prisoner has practised this species of theft on the open street, and no other, for a series of years, and managed by his dexterity of hand and swiftness of heel to make it pay pretty successfully.

GLASGOW SATURDAY POST   *23RD AUGUST 1845*

On Monday last, a labourer, named William Shearer, residing at Springburn, was charged at the Gorbals Police Court with having fraudulently obtained the sum of six pounds sterling, in the year 1842 from the managers of the Govan Colliery Society, on the pretence that his wife had died in Ireland. The regulations of the Society provide that the sum of six pounds shall be payable to members on the decease of a wife, but it has been ascertained since Shearer obtained this amount that his wife is still alive. The case having been remitted to the Justices, Shearer was yesterday tried, and on being found guilty sent sixty days to Bridewell.

GLASGOW SATURDAY POST   *3RD MARCH 1849*

One day at the end of last week a fiery faced little woman, named Mary Fitzgerald or Shearer, was brought before Bailie Smith at the Calton Police Court, on the charge of stealing two tartan shawls. From the evidence, it appeared that the prisoner had obtained access to the house in question for the purpose of 'reading the cups' or telling fortunes, and indeed, she is so well known in this capacity, that she goes by the name of the 'Spae wife of Calton'. The woman had committed the theft in the course of her professional visits. The witnesses were generally young girls who gave their testimony with a blush, evidently ashamed of their own credulity. Of course, they were promised affectionate husbands and families of children varying in number from eight to a dozen, with every earthly blessing in addition.

The case of theft was clearly proved, and the Magistrate resolved to prohibit the fortune-telling farce for two months, by sending the woman during that space to prison. Bailie Smith expressed the hope that the prophecy would turn out correct in the case of the pretty young girls, as they seemed doubtless sincere young creatures, who deserved good husbands.

GLASGOW EXAMINER   *7TH MARCH 1863*

David Taylor, chimneysweep, Spoutmouth, was fined £2 2s, or 40 days imprisonment, for placing a slate or stone on the chimney top of a house in Springbank on Monday. He said it was accidently done, but the Magistrate believed he had done it either out of mischief or in order to get a job.

PARTICK OBSERVER   *21ST DECEMBER 1877*

Catherine Martin, alias Grant, was sentenced to 10 days to prison for having stolen several doormats from houses in Church Street. It appears that Catherine's 'little game' had been to dress herself in a very 'respectable' way wearing a long waterproof cloak or ulster. She would then go boldly to the doors and lifting the mats conceal them under her cloak and walk off. From her appearance no one could suspect her of being a 'suspicious character'. She tried her game too often, however, the police 'dropped' on her, and she is now being entertained at the public expense for her cleverness.

ADVERTISER FOR AIRDRIE   6TH JANUARY 1883

At the Airdrie J.P. Court on Thursday — Messrs Neilson and Jack on the bench— two men belonging to Coatbridge, named James McKay and William Pollock, were convicted of theft of four hens and two cocks from a poultry house at Coatdyke. The theft was committed in a rather cunning way, and had the men not been known to the police as 'poultry fanciers' detection might not have been so easy. The real thief was a large dog, which the accused had trained to enter the poultry house, and after despatching a few fouls carry them in its mouth to where the men were stationed. The dog had done about a half dozen trips when the woman in charge of the poultry house was roused by the noise of the frightened poultry. The canine thief and his accomplices, however, got clear at the time, but owing to the reason stated the latter were apprehended, McKay was sentenced to 60 days imprisonment and Pollock to 30 days.

GLASGOW WEEKLY HERALD   30TH DECEMBER 1882

Christopher Larkin was accused of no fewer than nine different acts of theft committed in various places within the city from the 25th September till the 30th October, and on each occasion he stole a purse and money, the sums ranging from a sixpence up to 22s.

He pleaded guilty to five of the charges. It was explained the prisoner had practised what is known as the pigeon trick. He gained admission to the houses on the pretence that a pigeon belonging to him had escaped and was sitting either on the sill of the window or on the roof. His Lordship, addressing him said he must now go into penal servitude, and that for five years.

PARTICK STAR   *21ST APRIL 1894*

At Partick Police Court, on Thursday, James Morrison was charged with begging and threatening those who refused him alms. It was stated that Morrison had one of his arms in a sling, pretending something was wrong with it, but on Inspector McFarlane pulling it out it was found that the arm was all right. Bailie Crawford ordered accused to be fined one guinea, or ten days imprisonment.

GLASGOW WEEKLY MAIL   *21ST FEBRUARY 1885*

KILMARNOCK — At the Police Court on Wednesday, Thomas Dickson, pit sinker, Fore Street, pleaded guilty to begging in Croft Street on the 17th inst, and was sent eleven days to prison. He pretended to be dumb, and was using the dumb alphabet in his supplications, but when the Constable went to take it from him he quickly found speech, and gave him a hearty round of swearing.

GLASGOW WEEKLY MAIL   *2ND FEBRUARY 1895*

At the Dumbarton Sheriff Court, on Tuesday an English collier, named William Davis, pleaded not guilty to a charge of attempted fraud. The offence was committed in a pit at the Garscube Collieries, and is what is known among miners as 'pinning the hutches'. It is simply affixing tokens to hutches turned out by other miners, removing those attached, and thus getting credit for work done by others. Accused had been credited with eleven hutches on a shift when five was the average number, and eight were complained of as missing by other miners. Davis was sent to prison for fourteen days.

GLASGOW EVENING NEWS   *14TH JANUARY 1897*

Robert Lawson was charged at the Northern Police Court this morning with having fraudulently obtained a glass of whisky from a shop in Maitland

Street, the dodge whereby the liquor is obtained being popularly known as 'Shooting the Crow'.

Lawson, it was shown, asked for a glass of the best whisky they had in the shop, and after consuming it he decamped without paying. He was brought back when he offered a knife in payment which was declined. Lawson was convicted and sent to jail for seven days without option of fine.

Glasgow Weekly Herald   *30th January 1897*

Bailie R Anderson, who presided at the Southern Police Court on Tuesday, sent Hugh Killiet to prison for 14 days for the theft of two barrows between the 10th and 20th December last. Between the periods named Hugh had taken away two barrows, one from Nelson Street and the other from a back court off Mitchell Street, and after painting one of the barrows, he very cheekily took it and offered it for sale to the owner. It was only by the wheel that the owner discovered that he was being asked to buy his own property. He called the police, and the result was that Killiet was sent to prison for 14 days.

Glasgow Weekly Herald   *20th February 1897*

At Paisley Police Court, Charles Lynch, Candleriggs, Glasgow was charged with what in police phraseology, is known as 'duffing' or giving wrong information to a pawnbroker, while pawning a watch. He pleaded guilty, and was fined £1, or ten days in prison.

GLASGOW EVENING NEWS   *2ND MARCH 1897*

Robert Houston Wilson on Saturday night in Nuneaton Street was found with his hand in a drunk man's pocket. At the Eastern Police Court today Wilson was sent 60 days to prison.

GLASGOW WEEKLY MAIL   *22ND APRIL 1899*

John Christie, the young man who was recently sent to prison at Paisley for obtaining money from certain parties by representing that he had been bitten by their dogs, was on being liberated, immediately apprehended again by the local police, and brought on Monday before Bailie Munro in the Police Court, where two charges of a similar character were read against him. The frauds were committed on shopkeepers and the sums 6d and 1s, were of course to cover the doctor's fee. It was stated that Christie was wanted for similar frauds committed at Lenzie and Kirkintilloch. Bailie Munro passed sentence of 14 days imprisonment.

GLASGOW WEEKLY MAIL   *24TH JUNE 1899*

Francis Lafferty, boilermaker, pleaded guilty, at the Police Court on Monday to a charge of having on the previous day stolen a dog from a villa in Greenlaw Drive. Accused stated that he thought the animal was strayed. Bailie Allison, in passing sentence of five days imprisonment referred to the advertisements under 'Lost, Stolen or Strayed', the majority of which, in his opinion were inserted by dog thieves. You never hear, he said, of them finding a cat.

SPRINGBURN ADVERTISER   *9TH JANUARY 1902*

There is a practice having the name of 'Shooting the Crow', which is done by going into a public house and ordering a drink without having any money to pay for it. A man, named Wm. Smith, who resides in the Alexandra Parade, but who gave his address to the police as London Road, tried the game on in the public house of John McCrae, at 31 Parson Street. He ordered half pint of beer, drank it and made to walk out of the shop without paying for it. On being arrested and searched no money was found in his possession. Accused made the excuse that he was the worse of drink at the time, and did not know what he was doing. The Bailie passed sentence of 7s 6d or five days imprisonment.

GLASGOW HERALD   *31ST MARCH 1970*

Ellis Fraser (35), a patient at a drug addiction centre in London, arrived in Stirling on Saturday with 3s 1d in his pocket. To get a bed he feigned a heart attack.

At Stirling Sheriff Court yesterday Fraser, a factory cleaner, had sentence deferred until today for arrangements to be made to return him to the drug centre in London. Fraser pled guilty to having on Saturday, in Boroughmuir, Stirling, conducted himself in a disorderly manner by feigning a collapse and pretending to three persons that he was suffering from a heart attack, putting then into a state of fear and alarm. He also admitted fraudulently obtaining 15 milligrams of morphine, medical and hospital attention.

EVENING TIMES   *12TH JANUARY 1983*

Two Chinese waiters were fined £70 apiece who Fo Chung (23) admitted impersonating Kong Ho (20) and sitting a driving test in his place.

He admitted supporting Chung's deception when the Kirkcaldy waiters appeared at the town's Sheriff Court.

EVENING TIMES   *4TH APRIL 1986*

A Glasgow youth made a 'brief' appearance at Glasgow District Court on 'brief' charges when John Coulter, Camlachie, appeared before Stipendiary Magistrate Robin Christie.

He admitted stealing 100 packets of briefs from a store in Trongate. The briefs worth £149 were recovered. Mr Christie deferred sentence on Coulter for a social inquiry report.

The Guidmen

GLASGOW HERALD   *28TH DECEMBER 1832*

Adam Allan, John Hood and John Stewart, three very young blackguards, for stealing door-handles and bell-pulls were sentenced to seven years transportation. The rascals jocularly sung the stave of a thief song while leaving the dock commencing — 'Seven years time will soon wear awa'; and then we'll get hame in spite o' ye a'.'

GLASGOW ARGUS   *27TH JUNE 1833*

A young fellow was brought before the Magistrates on Friday, for being found lying drunk on the street at midnight, and vociferating with stentorian lungs 'Police, police!' On being questioned why he called for the police when no-one was annoying him, he replied with imperturable gravity, that 'he had called for them to help him up.' As it was his first offence, he was allowed to depart, but next time he will be made to pay porterage.

GLASGOW SATURDAY POST   *6TH JUNE 1844*

Issac Ewing, accused of the theft of a quantity of wearing apparel from a house in Drygate, Glasgow, pleaded not guilty. After the examination of witnesses he was found guilty. Sentence, 7 years transportation.

(This, it appears, is the eighth time the prisoner has been convicted in criminal courts). He did not appear to be more than 17 years of age and left the court whistling.

GLASGOW SATURDAY POST   *23RD OCTOBER 1847*

On Wednesday forenoon a master ropemaker, residing in Duke Street, was fined in the sum of two guineas, for an assault upon a night policeman on Monday evening. The most prominent feature in the assault was, walloping the policeman on the head with a cat which the assailant was carrying at the time.

GLASGOW EXAMINER   *27TH FEBRUARY 1858*

On Wednesday at the Central Police Court, a man named John Kerr, hailing from Gallowgate, was sentenced to 30 days imprisonment for having on Wednesday morning, while in a cell in the Central Police Office, stolen a pair of boots, a pair of socks, and a silk handkerchief, from the person of a man, named David Dobbie, who was confined in the same cell, on a charge of having been drunk and incapable.

GLASGOW EXAMINER   26TH DECEMBER 1863

John McDonald, a returned convict, was accused of having on Friday the 16th October last, stolen a topcoat from the door of the shop of Messrs Drummond & Leslie, clothiers and outfitters, Argyle Street. Panel pleaded not guilty, but after trial, he was convicted as libelled and sentenced to four years penal servitude. On receiving sentence the prisoner remarked: 'Thank you, My Lord, its not long to '67.'

HAMILTON ADVERTISER   14TH NOVEMBER 1868

Chess Rennie, collier, Waterloo, was accused of trying to overturn a house at Wishaw Cross. When in his cups or rather his cups in him, Charlie showed his valour, took hold of a two storey house and vowed he would throw it over. The police constable appearing at the time found that Charlie's threat was a vain boast and when brought before Bailie Shirlaw was fined for the threat the sum of 5s.

HAMILTON ADVERTISER   21ST NOVEMBER 1868

On Monday (before Provost Simpson) Thomas Lynch, Rumblingskyes forfeited the sum of 2s 6d by failing to appear; and James Miligan, residing in Byres Row, Wishaw forfeited 5s, these two being accused of doing nothing on the footpath and caught by the police constable in the act.

Hamilton Advertiser   *21st March 1874*

The greatest bully that Wishaw has seen for a long time appeared when Bill Murphy went swaggering down the street, threatening to eat everything that came before him. A boy from the blue-coat school proved too tough and Bill paid 15s rather than try to masticate a police constable.

Hamilton Advertiser   *27th February 1875*

On hearing talk of the gastronomic feats of 'Rab Ha's', Tam Dixon of Morningside, decided he could beat him all to sticks.

Having one night consumed most of the cooked meats in an eating house he seized and threatened to eat the Landlord. Tam thocht shame o' his threat, he left 10s at the local court and did not call back for his change.

HAMILTON ADVERTISER   *5TH JUNE 1875*

When Ned Davis' appetite was whetted one night with Old Glenlivet, he offered to fight every man in Kirk Road and eat half of the vanquished. Though cannibalistic in his acquirements, Ned cannot digest blue cloth. The sight of a Bob brought on the shakers, so that rather than lie in a bed in such close proximity to the lot of Blues, Ned staked and lost 15s.

ADVERTISER FOR AIRDRIE   *22ND MAY 1880*

William Stewart, a bricklayer, residing in High Street was charged with jostling and annoying foot passengers in the streets while in a state of utter intoxication. On account of William becoming a good customer to the Police, he was fined in the modified sum of 5s or 5 days.

HAMILTON ADVERTISER   *17TH DECEMBER 1881*

James Auchterlonie, miner, Young Street, was charged with shouting, swearing and offering to fight a door. Because the door could not, or did not reply in language as foul as the Jamsie man, he gave it a pounding with a hammer, for which he paid 12s 6d — clean cash.

It would appear that at least two of the worthy inhabitants of Bellshill, are desirous of a little more excitement than there has been for some time in the village, as witness a charge proved at the Airdrie J.P. Court against Edward Maclachlan, a labourer in Bellshill and his wife Ann, of assault and breach of the peace by using party expressions. These two personages had got on the 'spree' last Saturday evening and very late called on Widow Black in Fairys Land, and treated her and her daughter to a round of the choicest 'party cries'. Edward Maclachlan then assaulted the widow in the most brutal manner, his 'better half' at the same time attending to the daughter. By this time half the village was turned out, but Inspector Grant of the 'Blues' appeared on the scene and apprehended Maclachlan and his wife. They were brought before Mr Frank Murray and Provost Black at Airdrie on Monday, and as stated above were convicted. Edward was fined in 21s or 10 days imprisonment while Ann was let off with 10s 6d or 5 days. It would also appear that Ann is treasurer as her fine was promptly paid.

ADVERTISER FOR AIRDRIE   5TH AUGUST 1882

It would appear that at least two of the worthy inhabitants of Bellshill, are desirous of a little more excitement than has been for some time in the village, as witness a charge proved at the Airdrie J.P. Court against Edward Maclachlan, a labourer in Bellshill and his wife Ann, of assault and breach of the peace by using party expressions These two personages had got on the 'spree' last Saturday evening and very late called on Widow Black in Fairys Land, and treated her and her daughter to a round of the choicest 'party cries'. Edward Maclachlan then assaulted the widow in the most brutal manner, his 'better half' at the same time attending to the daughter. By this time half the village was turned out, but Inspector Grant of the 'Blues' appeared on the scene and apprehended Maclachlan and his wife. They were brought before Mr Frank Murray and Provost Black at Airdrie on Monday, and as stated above were convicted. Edward was fined in 21s or 10 days imprisonment while Ann was left off with 10s 6d or 5 days. It would also appear that Ann is treasurer as her fine was promptly paid, while the 'good man' went downstairs.

GLASGOW WEEKLY HERALD   *24TH MARCH 1883*

GREENOCK — James Beaton, a carpenter, was convicted at Monday's Police Court of jostling passengers in Cathcart Square and Hamilton Street on Saturday. It seems that when James gets a 'dram' he has a habit of pushing people off the pavement with his shoulder and hustling them about generally. He had been sixteen times previously convicted of the same offence. The Magistrate ordered him to pay a fine of 20s, or 14 days imprisonment remarking at the same time that Beaton had now been fined in the aggregate sum of £24 for these offences.

WISHAW PRESS & ADVERTISER   *10TH JANUARY 1885*

A special Court was held on Saturday, Bailie Thomson on the bench. James Kerr, Cambusnethan was charged with assaulting and kicking his wife. From the evidence it appeared that when his wife went to the well for water she saw her husband with his arms round a girl's neck and kissing her. This she resented by emptying the water on him. He called on a passing friend to knock her down, which he obliged him by doing. Kerr then kicked her severely. There being other previous convictions he was fined 40s or 30 days.

WISHAW PRESS & ADVERTISER   *11TH JULY 1885*

A boy named Thomas Connelly, 14 years of age, pleaded guilty to a charge of malicious mischief and was fined 2s 6d or 24 hours imprisonment. On the 27th of last month, he, for a bit of diversion, dropped a grocer's ledger down an old woman's chimney and broke her teapot. The house was filled with smoke and soot, and the occupant — an octogenarian — nearly frightened to death.

GLASGOW WEEKLY MAIL   *14TH NOVEMBER 1885*

KILMARNOCK — At the Sheriff Court, Thomas Barland, miner, Orchard Street, Galston, was charged with theft. After evidence, the jury unanimously found Barland guilty as libelled. The Sheriff, referring to the three previous convictions against Barland, said he seemed a hardened criminal, and could not sentence him to less than one year's imprisonment. A woman thought to be his wife, cried, 'Ye're nailed, Tam! Keep up your heart!'

POLLOCKSHAWS NEWS   *28TH NOVEMBER 1885*

George McKnacher, tramway car driver, who was last week fined for assaulting Constable Brown, was at this court charged with using threatening language towards Constables Lawson and Stewart on Saturday last. He told the officers he could 'do' for the lot of them, and said that nothing would give him more pleasure than to pay a few pounds as fines for assaulting Constables. Accused failed to appear, and forfeited a pledge of £1.

MOTHERWELL TIMES   *24TH JULY 1886*

Robert McNaught, puddler of King Street was taking a 'rise' out of himself on Saturday 10th July in King Street. He quarrelled with himself and began

101

to use big words and latterly fought it out with himself. Who comes off victorious has not yet been published but we suspect Bob would be second man. It being illegal to quarrel and fight with one's self and especially dangerous of knocking out one's eyelashes and of peeling the bark of one's nasal organ his honour fined Bob 7s 6d or five days imprisonment.

AIRDRIE ADVERTISER   *4TH SEPTEMBER 1886*

On Thursday, at the Airdrie J.P. Court, before Mr J.M.Ormiston and Dr Mack, John McGrath, residing at the Old Forge at Calderbank, and who apparently thinks himself a bit of a pugilist, was brought up on a charge of having stripped himself in regular prize ring style, and challenged anyone to come and fight. He had fortified himself pretty well beforehand, and was so loud in his boasting that his challenge was not accepted, except by Henry Lewis, a public protector of the peace, who not only 'squared off' the 'bold McGrath', but with the aid of the two Justices on the bench compelled him to leave half-a-sovereign for the benefit of the funds of the court, and a warning to aspiring pugilists.

GOVAN PRESS   *6TH AUGUST 1887*

A wife assault charge was served against Lauchlan McFadyen, Govan Road, whose spouse was unable to attend, and on bail of £2 2s he was liberated till Wednesday. While leaving the court he was heard to say that there was nothing wrong with his wife, 'just lying drunk she was.'

WISHAW PRESS   *10TH MARCH 1888*

Anthony McDonald ironworker, Berryhill, was con-victed of malicious mischief. On Monday afternoon, nearly opposite the Distillery, he had accosted Edward Burns, labourer, Craigneuk, and kicked the tin box containing his 'piece' from under his arm by which he was prevented from going to his work. McDonald was convicted and fined 10s or 7 days imprisonment.

GOVAN PRESS   *22ND SEPTEMBER 1888*

John Coffell, who resides in Helen Street, Govan, is minus 15s which he had in his possession on Satur-day night. It appears that Mr Coffell and a friend were up Plantation way on that evening and were eating apples. As they came near Craighall Street, John saw a policeman standing there. The temptation to have a shot seemed to be too much for him for he threw an apple and struck the policeman on the mouth. 'Robert' objected to the forcible attempt to put the apple down his throat, so he took John along to the Police Station and at the Police Court on Monday morning Baille Kirkwood ordered Mr Coffell to pay a fine of 15s or go to prison for ten days. The fine was paid.

RUTHERGLEN REFORMER   *28TH MARCH 1890*

Denis Martin, labourer, Coats Street, pleaded 'almost not guilty' of breach of the peace in Dunbeth Road on Saturday night. He was found altogether guilty and fined 10s, or five days.

MOTHERWELL TIMES   *12TH JULY 1890*

Hugh Love, miner, Windmillhill Street, pleaded guilty to assaulting a constable while in the execution of his duty by striking him on the head with a cabbage. He was fined 2s 6d or twenty four hours.

SOUTH SUBURBAN PRESS   *29TH AUGUST 1891*

At Plantation Police Court on Monday, Chas Sime, a young man, pleaded guilty to creating a disturbance near Paisley Road on Saturday night. Provost McLean asked where he belonged to and on being informed that he came from Glasgow, he said 'if he is a Glasgow man, we'll give him a light fine, 7s 6d or four days'.

Donald Kennedy, a beggar, hailing from Argyleshire, was charged at the Queens Park Police Court on Saturday, with having been found begging in Mount Florida, the previous day. Donald on being asked to plead, said that for all he got in Mount Florida, it was scarcely worth going up the brae for. He was admonished.

Joseph McDermott, labourer, for assaulting Peter Strachan, eating-house keeper, with a black pudding, was fined 10s 6d or seven days.

At the Paisley Sheriff Court yesterday — Honorary Sheriff Substitute Dunn on the bench — Alexander Graham was charged with having on 16th July, in Main Street, Barrhead, assaulted a fish hawker by striking him on the head with a bell. He pleaded guilty and was fined 21s with the alternative of one month's imprisonment.

James Gordon, labourer and Peter McNulty, billposter, both residing in Holmes Street, Hamilton, were accused of indecently staggering under the influence of liquor in Main Street the previous day. Gordon pleaded guilty, but McNulty denied the charge, pointing out that he was endeavouring to assist his companion home when taken into custody. The evidence of the constables, however, went to show that both men were intoxicated at the time of their apprehension and that McNulty, instead of trying to assist his comrade home appeared to be making tracks for the nearest hotel. The prisoner stoutly denied this impeachment, and, evidently as conclusive proof of his sobriety at the time, exclaimed, 'Did I no' staun on one leg efter being brought to the office?'

The Fiscal stated that McNulty on being taken to the cells described himself as the chief editor and part-partner of a well known local paper, which, jocularly remarked the Fiscal, was surely sufficient evidence that the man was drunk.

Accused: 'No your Honour; I'm the bill poster of the establishment, but I can fill any position inside the office.'

The charge was found proven and a fine of 10s each or seven days imprisonment was imposed.

GLASGOW WEEKLY HERALD   *10TH SEPTEMBER 1892*

At Wishaw Police Court on Monday, Edward Beards, ironworker, was charged with having, in the Excelsior Ironworks, Shieldmuir, assaulted another ironworker, bearing the singular name of River Jordan. The Fiscal (Mr Burgess) said it was recorded in biblical history that Elisha with Elijah's mantle smote the River Jordan and past over it, but in this case the accused smote River Jordan on the mouth and knocked him down. He was fined 15s or ten days.

IRVINE — At a special Burgh Police Court yesterday — Bailie Wilson on the bench — William Grubb, David McMeechan, Robert Hunter, Samuel Elliot, James McMurtrie and John Reid were charged with having on Monday night 19th September committed a breach of the peace in Bridgegate. The accused, who are Operative Bakers pleaded not guilty; and were defended by Mr Alexander D Young, Solicitor.

Mr John Currie, Baker, Montgomery Street, stated in evidence that at the public house of Mr Newall, in Bridgegate, where he had stopped his van, and where two of his men were having a pint of beer, he had been molested, and his horse frightened by the accused and others 'booing' and shouting at him. This evidence was generally corroborated by two of Mr Currie's men and his two sons who were present. When asked in cross-examination how many people were on top of the van, Mr Currie caused a good deal of laughter in court by replying somewhat humourously that there were three people and himself which made four, and the horse that made five. A number of other witnesses testified to the accused having taken no part whatever in the alleged disturbance and the charge against the whole of the men was dismissed as not proven.

Daniel Boyle, labourer, Dovecot, for pretending to be drunk in Main Street on Saturday night, and jostling the people on the pavement, was fined 30s or twenty days.

AIRDRIE ADVERTISER   *18TH MARCH 1893*

Before Bailie Aitken in the Burgh Court — James Robertson, a pedlar of no fixed abode, was charged with having stolen a gentleman's tweed overcoat from the dwelling-house at 65 High Street, occupied by Mr J.C. Miller, painter. The prisoner pleaded guilty, and was sentenced to fifteen days imprisonment.

Prisoner: "Thank you honour, the snow'll be a' awa', when I come out.'

SOUTH SUBURBAN PRESS   *8TH JULY 1893*

At the Queen's Park Police Court on Monday 'Jamie' Campbell, a well known Govanhill sweep, admitted to Judge J H Martin that he behaved himself in a very obstreperous manner in Cathcart Road on the evening of Saturday 24th June, and used abusive language to a brother-in-trade. The Magistrate, after considering the case, said he would allow James to go with a small fine this time, on condition that he would see to the mending of his ways in future. This he readily agreed to do, and a fine of 10s 6d or 8 days was imposed. 'Jamie' cast a contemptuous glance at the 'limb of the law' and left the court in a manner which betokened his surprise at the Magistrate's estimation of leniency.

George Jenkins was found sleeping in a box at the goods station of the N.B.R. at Ruchill on Sunday morning. George, who has been before designated the 'King of the Maryhill loafers', as dirty and unkempt as ever, was sent to prison for 14 days.

At Dumbarton Police Court on Tuesday, a vagrant named James Mullen was fined 5s or three days for being drunk and disorderly. His clothing was by no means scarce, as he wore two jackets, three vests, seven shirts, two mufflers and three pairs of drawers, besides other ordinary wearing apparel.

At Govan Police Court on Wednesday — Bailie Campbell on the bench — A young lad named Samuel Irvine was charged with having stolen three pounds of tobacco, 3s in money and a pair of trousers. Accused pleaded guilty to stealing the tobacco only. The Fiscal asked conviction on one charge and stated that the accused had been several times convicted of theft. Irvine was sentenced to thirty days imprisonment. On hearing his sentence, accused shouted to someone in the Court, 'So long, Geordie!'

Before Bailie Crawford at the Partick Police Court on Monday, John Herd, labourer, 18 Muirhead Street,

Partick, was charged with a serious assault on a man named Robert White, whom he struck on the head with a large jug, subsequently kicking him. William Pearson stated that he was present when the man Herd was assaulted.

The Clerk: 'What was the first thing that occurred after you and White went into the house?'

Witness: 'Well, the first thing was White pawned his shirt and sent for a bucket of beer.'

The Magistrate commented on the serious nature of the assault. Herd might have killed the man altogether, and he could not impose a lighter sentence than 30 days in prison without option of fine.

SOUTH SUBURBAN PRESS   *26TH MAY 1894*

Thomas Cranshaw, shiprigger, residing at 39 Smith Street, was fined 10s 6d with the option of spending a week 'up by' for having on Saturday last committed a breach of the peace in a shop in Sussex Street, and assaulted the shopman.

GLASGOW WEEKLY HERALD   *8TH DECEMBER 1894*

At Edinburgh Police Court — John McFarlane (21) dairyman, 41 Scotland Street, Edinburgh was handed over to the parochial authorities as insane, he having attempted to commit suicide by exploding 4d worth of gunpowder under his head.

GLASGOW WEEKLY MAIL   28TH JULY 1895

Noah planted a vineyard, and he drank of the wine and was drunken. All the days of Noah were nine hundred and fifty years. John Jack emulated the Captain of the Ark in so far as he got drunken. We would not be wishing John well if we expressed the hope that he would also successfully emulate him as regards length of life.

John: 'It is quite true.'

Magistrate: 'Seven and six or five days.'

John walked away with the aspect of one who has shied a wooden ball at a 'Kokay nut' and missed.

SOUTH SUBURBAN PRESS   2ND FEBRUARY 1895

Charles Malloy, a youth with a grimy face and a leering smile, was called to give evidence in a car versus lorry case heard at Queens Park Police court on Friday. Charles had been driving a lemonade cart across the tramway when a car came down the hill, and smashed into the rear of his lorry, throwing him and the vanman to the ground, and damaging the vehicle. Cross-examined by Mr Johnstone: 'When did you see the car?'

'I didn't see the car till I was nearly over the rails.'

'You might have seen it if you had been looking.'

'Could I watch two cars?' *(laughter)*

'Where were you?'

'Where was I? *(laughter)* I was half across the rail.'

'Were you going fast?'

'The horse was walking.'

'Couldn't you have hurried up?'

'Aye, but the horse wadna' hurry up!' *(laughter)*

'Did you try to hurry it up?'

'Aye, *(laughter)* I hit it wi' the reins.'

'Where was your master, or superior officer?'

'The man that sells the stuff?' *(laughter)* He couldna' see me, he was standing at the back.'

'But he could see the car?'

'I don't know whether he could or no'.' *(laughter)*

'Could you see him?'

'No. I couldna' look at him, and look at the car.' *(great laughter)*

'I did not ask you that. Could you have seen him if you had wanted to?'

'It would have been as much as I could do.'

'Don't waste the time of the Court. Are you the regular driver?'

'Yes.'

In summing up the case, Mr Johnstone referred to witness as the most irresponsible driver he had ever seen in charge of a vehicle on the public street, and thought the recklessness was entirely on his part.

The lad's employer rose to speak to Malloy's capacity as a driver but he was not heard. The car driver was convicted of reckless driving and fined 7s 6d or 5 days.

RUTHERGLEN REFORMER   *9TH OCTOBER 1896*

Edward O'Neil, labourer, Bank Street, was charged with having on Saturday night, the 3rd inst, created a breach of the peace within the Theatre Royal. Chief Constable Anderson explained that accused had been watching the progress of the play, and at a certain stage in the proceedings had taken off his boots and thrown them on to the stage with the object of striking the villain. The Bailie imposed a fine of 15s or ten days.

GLASGOW EVENING NEWS   *6TH AUGUST 1897*

A Greenock man got totally drunk and incapable twice in one day and has been fined 7s 6d for the feat.

GLASGOW EVENING NEWS   *6TH AUGUST 1897*

The police have added 10s 6d to this week's bill of a Govan lodger who threw his landlady downstairs.

GOVAN PRESS   *21ST AUGUST 1897*

Robert Scott, a middle-aged man, an engineer keeper to trade, residing at 14½ Houston Street was before Bailie Storrie at the Police Court on Tuesday charged with having created a breach of the peace, struck a goat, and assaulted it's owner, a coal dealer in St James' Street, on the previous Monday. Accused pled guilty and was fined 7s 6d or five days

GLASGOW EVENING NEWS   *14TH JANUARY 1898*

At Govan Police Court this morning Bailie Hutcheson on the bench, a youth, John Morran (16) was sentenced to 30 days imprisonment for having stolen a silver watch and silver albert from his father's house at 29 John Street, yesterday afternoon. As the accused was being led from court, he shouted to his father:

'When I come out I will knock your brains out!' The magistrate ordered him to be brought back and increased the sentence to 60 days imprisonment.

PARTICK & MARYHILL PRESS　　　　　29TH APRIL 1898

Bernard Gillespie, who resides in 28 Newton Street, looked rather dejected as he stood at the bar once more on Monday morning. He acknowledged having been disorderly in Dumbarton Road near Kelvin Street on Saturday night and in answer to Bailie Wood he said he had nothing to say.

Bailie Wood: 'It is a hopeless case.'

Accused: 'Yes.'

Assessor: 'I thought when you got a chance the last time you were never to be here again.'

Accused: 'I thought so too.'

Superintendent McAndrew: 'He has been temperate for 4 months.'

Accused said if he was let off this time he would never come back again.

Bailie Wood: 'That is what you always say.'

Accused (earnestly): 'If I come back next time you can shoot me.' *(laughter)*

Sentence 10s 6d or 7 days.

GLASGOW WEEKLY HERALD　　　　　29TH JULY 1898

Edward and Thomas Docherty, labourers, Commercial Street, were at Dundee on Monday charged with fighting with each other on Saturday night. They pleaded guilty.

The Magistrate: 'Are you twins?'

Accused: 'We are.'

The Magistrate: 'What were you quarrelling about?'

The Prosecutor: 'They were disputing as to who was the better man.'

The Magistrate: 'That's very funny. They will have to pay 15s each.'

GOVAN PRESS   *16TH SEPTEMBER 1898*

At Police Court on Monday — Bailie McMillan on the bench — a labourer named John Boyle, residing in Rutland House, was charged with having assaulted a woman named Mrs McCulloch. It appeared that the accused had been worse for drink and had gone to see the woman in question. On arriving at the house he immediately proposed marriage and on her refusing to have anything to do with him he gave her a thrashing. Boyle pleaded guilty and was fined 15s with alternative of 10 days imprisonment.

PARTICK STAR   *3RD DECEMBER 1898*

Two coalmen named Peter Currie and John Fallow were charged with having quarelled and fought in Gardner Street on 23rd November. It seems that Fallow was imitating Currie's father because he did not cry 'coal, coal', but 'whales, whales'. Currie, junr, resented this conduct, and the quarrel began. The magistrate said they could not be allowed to settle their disputes in that manner, and fined them each 5s or 3 days imprisonment.

A negro named William Oatts, described as a labourer, having no fixed place of abode was accused of making use of obscene language in the early hours of Sunday morning. He pleaded guilty.

The Fiscal: 'Can you write your name?'

Accused (promptly): 'Can't write.'

The Fiscal: 'What country are you?'

Accused: 'America'.

It was stated that the accused, being destitute committed the offence in order to obtain a night's shelter. On being sentenced to pay 20s or suffer fourteen days imprisonment he remarked: 'I'll have a bed now for a bit.'

Peter McLauchlan, a vanman, of 14 Bell Street, Calton, was charged at the Queen's Park Police Court on Wednesday with having in Battlefield Avenue been guilty of furious driving whereby he knocked down and partly destroyed a wooden fence adjoining the road there. He pled guilty and was fined 21s or 14 days imprisonment. It seems that a number of ducks had been crossing the road at the time and McLauchlan had urged the horse after them with the object of preventing them from making their escape through the fence referred to. He was too keen, however, and ran down the fence instead. The ducks escaped.

WISHAW PRESS   *20TH MAY 1899*

Three youths answering to the names of John Linnan, labourer, English Buildings, Sheildmuir, John Donnelly, ironworker and Duncan Doyle, hammer driver, Cowies Square, Craigneuk pleaded guilty to a charge of annoying the lieges of Cowies Square by playing pitch and toss. The Fiscal stated that several complaints had been made to the police about young men playing pitch and toss in the public square, especially on Sunday.

The Assessor: 'Was this on Sunday?'

The Fiscal: 'No it was on Saturday — the Jewish Sunday.'

A fine of 5s or 3 days imprisonment was imposed.

WISHAW PRESS   *24TH JULY 1899*

John Anderson, miner, Belhaven Old Row, Craigneuk, pleaded guilty to having behaved in a drunk and disorderly manner in Kerr and Mitchell Square. It seemed that he was first warned by the police as to his reprehensible conduct. When they saw him again, he was enquiring for them with a brick in his hand, and declared in choice language what would happen when they met. He was fined 10s or 7 days imprisonment.

GLASGOW WEEKLY MAIL   *19TH AUGUST 1899*

At the Burgh Police Court on Monday, Provost Stewart heard a case in which a wedding was disturbed by an unfortunate incident. It was a charge of assault made against the best man, James Paul, lorryman, East End, who, it was alleged, had thrown a tacketed boot out of the window of the carriage which was conveying the wedding party to the festivities, and injured Elizabeth Middleton, pottery worker. Paul stated that it was not a nice thing, for a wedding party to have such a boot beside them while they were going to the ministers.

The Provost: 'Did you not know the boot was for good luck?'

In the circumstances the accused was dismissed. The Provost advised him not to be so reckless the next marriage he officiated at.

PARTICK & MARYHILL PRESS   *20TH APRIL 1900*

Wm Heap, hailing from Lambhill, was arrested on Tuesday about one o'clock and taken to the Police Office in a helpless state of intoxication. About eight o'clock he was allowed out on a pledge of 7s 6d. He stated that he worked on the night shift and was anxious to start work at ten o'clock. Two hours afterwards he was again picked off the street in a helpless condition and taken to the police office. Early next morning he left another pledge of 7s 6d and departed.

GLASGOW WEEKLY MAIL   *12TH MAY 1900*

At the Sheriff Court on Monday, John Dick, moulder, Camelon was charged with stealing a metal cattle-feeding trough from Carmuirs Farms. Accused said he supposed he was guilty, but he was not in the habit of stealing. He had been drinking, and was fairly in the blues.

Accused said: 'I just came out of jail this morning for jumping into the Forth and Clyde Canal, and that was not a wise man's trick.'

The Sheriff sent him back to prison again for 14 days.

Springburn Advertiser   *24th May 1900*

When the Court Officer at St Rollox Police Court on Monday shouted 'John Kent, Hugh Gilroy!', the former, badly scratched about the nose, and the latter, son of Erin, stepped forward to the bar — The charge — fighting with each other in Springburn Road on Saturday night — having been read, both pleaded not guilty. Police evidence was then given, at the close of which Kent said 'I had jist left a refreshment bar an' wis wipin' ma lips wi' a Union Jack hankey I had, when a crowd of young fellas began bowing at me. Fur a lark,I gied the hankey a bit wave, when this chap here took it oot o' ma' haun', stamped on it, an' nearly pu'ed the nose aff ma face.' *(loud laughter)* 'Whit are ye laffin' at? Here's the marks yet.' *(renewed laughter)*

Gilroy: 'Did yez not troi tew wipe me nose wid your handerkerchief?' *(laughter)*

Kent: 'Me! — never.' *(laughter)*

Bailie Cleland: 'You are each fined 15s with the alternative of 14 days imprisonment.'

Henry McCartney, coal carrier, a notable local worthy, was brought up at the Police Court on Monday charged with creating a breach of the peace. This was his 107th appearance at the bar and Bailie Smith fined him 15s with the option of ten days.

John Carter, against whom five previous convictions were recorded appeared at St Rollox Police Court on Monday — before Police Judge J. H. Martin — charged with assaulting a Constable in Garneed Road. He had been conducting himself in a disorderly manner, and when two policemen arrested him he committed the assault. On hearing the sentence — thirty days imprisonment pronounced, he whistled and walked to the cell with a braggart look.

Wm Cruikshank, moulder, Victoria Street, Newmains, was charged with throwing snowballs, in Main Street on Saturday night. He pleaded guilty. The Fiscal stated that from the information of the police he found that the accused was 'capering' about in the street. Some companions of the accused passed and he lifted and compressed two handfuls of snow. He missed his companions in throwing the snowballs and two ladies were nearly hit. The police said there was a good deal of this horseplay but he (the Fiscal) did not know why they called it horseplay, as horses did not throw snowballs. The Bailie imposed a fine of 2s 6d with the alternative of two days imprisonment.

POLLOCKSHAWS NEWS   *9TH SEPTEMBER 1904*

Three young men named David Dow, engineer, 25 Rossendale Road, Scott Paterson, machineman, 16 Maxwell Street, and James Kyle, machineman, 19 Matilda Street, were charged with creating a breach of the peace. The accused had been drinking.

Bailie Baird (to Kyle): 'If you are drunk at 19, what will you be at 49?'

Kyle: 'Drunker.'

Bailie Baird said he was shocked at such a reply. The accused were each fined 2s 6d or imprisonment for three days.

PARTICK & MARYHILL PRESS   *18TH AUGUST 1905*

Henry McCartney, described as a coalcarrier, of no fixed residence made his 147th appearance in Govan Police Court on Monday morning and pleaded guilty to a charge of being drunk and incapable. He said he had got a little light in the head. 'You have got that way nearly 150 times' said the Prosecutor (Mr Dykes). Accused asked to be allowed to go home to County Derry where he thought he could pick himself up. He left there when he was seven. Sentence of £2 or a month's imprisonment was passed.

Partick & Maryhill Press   15th December 1905

The colour of a man's socks figured largely in a case of assault that was heard at Plantation Police Court on Monday before Police Judge Wightman. It appeared from the evidence that they had been displayed offensively, for their colour was designed to irritate the religious feelings of the viewee. A picture of a 'man on horseback' as one of the female witnesses described it, which hung in the complainer's house appeared also to have caused the accused some annoyance. 'King William crossing the Boyne' said the Assessor (Mr Houston). Complainer admitted that the picture represented the historical incident referred to by Mr Houston, but denied that he had drawn the attention of the accused to it. Police Judge Wightman found charge of assault proven and passed sentence of 10s 6d or 7 days.

Motherwell Times   11th December 1908

John Terris, a Pole, Oakfield Place was fined in 25s or fourteen days for assaulting another Pole with a stick.

Motherwell Times   22nd September 1916

George Henderson, miner, Coatbridge, pled guilty to committing a nuisance on Saturday night. He was worse for drink.

Bailie Coughtrie (to the accused): 'If you were going to commit a nuisance, do it in Coatbridge, but don't come to the Burgh of Motherwell.' The penalty is £2 or fifteen days.

MOTHERWELL TIMES   *16TH FEBRUARY 1917*

John Murray, labourer, Park Street House pled guilty to attempting to enter a public house while in a drink-intoxicated condition. The accused was fined in £2 or fifteen days.

Mr Burns to accused: 'Have you got the money?'

Accused: 'No.'

Mr Burns: 'Have you no money at all?'

Accused: 'Well, I've got 10 pennies.'

Mr Burns: 'You'll be wanting time to pay. How long do you want?'

Accused: 'Twelve years.'

Accused was allowed a fortnight to pay.

MOTHERWELL TIMES   *30TH OCTOBER 1931*

Thomas Wyllie, miner, Shields Road, Motherwell, admitted stealing potatoes and was fined £2 or twenty days imprisonment. A friend of the accused paid the fine and coolly asked if he could now claim the potatoes at the police station. The Fiscal sharply rebuked the man for his audacity and the incident which evoked some merriment then closed.

GOVAN PRESS   *17TH MAY 1940*

Pleading guilty to having on a Saturday from a ship in Princess Dock stolen three gills of whisky, George Black (29) was fined one guinea or 14 days imprisonment. Accused told Bailie John Duffy the whisky came from a leaking case. 'It was a pity to see good stuff going to waste,' he added.

'I was singing *Here comes the Factor* and *Bee-Baw Babbity* in a back court in Govan when a man gave me a couple of coppers and I don't remember anymore.' So said James McLean (42) of no fixed abode, when he appeared in the local court on a drunk and incapable charge and tendered a plea of not guilty. According to two police witnesses the part that James forgot was that he was found lying in a helpless state in Jura Street, reeking of methylated spirits and had to be bodily carried to a police van.

Said James: 'I was weak, not drunk, and if your honour will give me a chance I have a home to go to 'though I am the black sheep of the family.'

Said the Fiscal: 'The accused states that he is the black sheep of the family and in order that he return to the fold a sheep of a lighter colour, I would ask you honour to impose a term of imprisonment so that he can have attention.'

A fine of 10s with alternative of eight days imprisonment was imposed, and when the Fiscal opposed time to pay James said: 'I could get it inside an hour by singing in the backcourt.'

A man charged on Monday, at Govan Police Court, admitted being drunk, but denied being incapable on Saturday. 'I was drunk,' he told the court, 'but that was the only matter.' Two policemen said they found him hanging to a Belisha beacon. Asked by Bailie A.M. Stewart why he was hanging to the beacon, accused replied: '...because I could not stand'. Not having any previous conviction, the Magistrate said: 'I will let you off with a fine of 10s.'

EVENING CITIZEN   *11TH JANUARY 1972*

A Lanarkshire pensioner made his 129th court appearance today only 24 hours after his 128th. In the dock was William McLinton (66), Blantyre, who has spent 11 years in prison and paid more than £100 in fines since 1922. An agent told the court: 'Once this person has started drinking he cannot stop.' Sheriff Ian Dickson jailed McLinton for 3 months.

EVENING CITIZEN   *28TH AUGUST 1972*

A man who was stated to have been advised to change to drinking diabetic beer instead of normal beer to help him lose weight was fined £40 and disqualified from driving for a year at Stirling Sheriff Court today. Andrew Bennie pleaded guilty to driving a car when the quantity of alcohol in his blood was in excess of the prescribed limit. An agent said that Bennie had been advised by his doctor to lose weight.

GOVAN PRESS   *29TH MARCH 1974*

A young Pollock streaker appeared at Glasgow Central Police Court on Monday was asked by Stipendiary Magistrate T. McLaughlin: 'Do you think you should see a doctor? There might be a little kink somewhere.' The court was told that George Todd, Pollok, who admitted a breach of the peace and two previous convictions, had been seen running naked along Renfield Street, West Regent Street and West Nile Street on Saturday night. He was fined £20.

Evening Times   *12th January 1984*

A big-hearted bandit who snatched almost £300 at knifepoint from a shop till handed back some of the money to the terrified woman manageress and said 'Keep that for a tip.'

But the raider's gesture did not pay off when he appeared for sentence at the High Court in Edinburgh today. Lord Wheatley jailed 22-year-old William Lamb, Edinburgh, for four years.